D0125143

Teens at Risk

Stephen P. Thompson, Book Editor

GREENHAVEN PRESS
A part of Gale, Cengage Learning

GALE
CENGAGE Learning·

Detroit • New York • San Francisco • New Haven, Conn • Waterville, Maine • London

Elizabeth Des Chenes, *Director, Publishing Solutions*

© 2013 Greenhaven Press, a part of Gale, Cengage Learning

Gale and Greenhaven Press are registered trademarks used herein under license.

For more information, contact:
Greenhaven Press
27500 Drake Rd.
Farmington Hills, MI 48331-3535
Or you can visit our Internet site at gale.cengage.com.

For product information and technology assistance, contact us at:

Gale Customer Support, 1-800-877-4253.
For permission to use material from this text or product, submit all requests online at www.cengage.com/permissions.

Further permissions questions can be emailed to permissionrequest@cengage.com.

Articles in Greenhaven Press anthologies are often edited for length to meet page requirements. In addition, original titles of these works are changed to clearly present the main thesis and to explicitly indicate the author's opinion. Every effort is made to ensure that Greenhaven Press accurately reflects the original intent of the authors. Every effort has been made to trace the owners of copyrighted material.

Cover image © Helder Almeida/Shutterstock.com.

LIBRARY OF CONGRESS CATALOGING-IN-PUBLICATION DATA

Teens at risk / Stephen P. Thompson, book editor.
p. cm. -- (Opposing viewpoints)
Includes bibliographical references and index.
ISBN 978-0-7377-6430-7 (hbk.) -- ISBN 978-0-7377-6431-4 (pbk.)
1. Problem youth--United States. 2. Juvenile delinquency--United States.
3. Teenage pregnancy--United States. I. Thompson, Stephen P., 1953-
HV1431.T446 2013
362.7083--dc23

2012032404

Printed in the United States of America
1 2 3 4 5   17 16 15 14 13

Contents

Why Consider Opposing Viewpoints?   11

Introduction   14

Chapter 1: What Factors Put Teens at Risk?

Chapter Preface   18

1. Risk Taking Is a Positive Function of the
   Teenage Brain   20
   David Dobbs

2. Teen Food Options Promote Obesity and
   Poor Health   30
   Eric A. Finkelstein and Laurie Zuckerman

3. Cyber Junkie: Escape the Gaming and Internet Trap   37
   Kevin Roberts

4. Violent Video Games Promote Teen Aggression
   and Violence   43
   Craig A. Anderson

5. Violent Video Games Do Not Promote Teen
   Aggression and Violence   52
   Serena Gordon

Periodical and Internet Sources Bibliography   56

Chapter 2: How Does Substance Abuse Impact Teens?

Chapter Preface   58

1. Teen Substance Use Often Leads to Addiction   60
   National Center on Addiction and Substance Abuse

2. Teen Substance Use Seldom Leads to Addiction 70
   Jann Gumbiner

3. Marijuana Use Is Harmful   74
   National Institute on Drug Abuse

4. Teens Are Choosing Marijuana over More Harmful
   Substances   82
   Kristen Gwyne

5. The Minimum Legal Drinking Age Should
   Be Lowered   90
   Michelle Minton

6. The Minimum Legal Drinking Age Should Not
   Be Lowered   95
   Carla T. Main

Periodical and Internet Sources Bibliography   103

Chapter 3: Does Sexuality Put Teens at Risk?

Chapter Preface   105

1. Sexual Harassment Pervasive in US Middle and
   High Schools, Survey Finds   107
   David Crary

2. Poll: Young People Say Online Meanness Pervasive   111
   CBS News

3. Teen Sex Education Should Emphasize Abstinence
   Until Marriage   117
   Alean Zeiler

4. Teen Sex Education Should Emphasize Protection
   and Safety   126
   Patrick Malone and Monica Rodriguez

Periodical and Internet Sources Bibliography   136

Chapter 4: How Should Society Deal with Teen Discipline and Teen Crime?

Chapter Preface   138

1. Bullying of Gay Teens Is a Serious Problem   139
   Kenneth Miller

2. Teenage Bullying Should Not Be Treated as a Crime   **148**
  Jessica Bennett

3. Juvenile Detention Is an Ineffective Teen Sentencing
  Policy   **156**
  Richard A. Mendel/The Annie E. Casey Foundation

4. Problems with Zero Tolerance Policies Have Been
  Exaggerated   **163**
  Ken Trump

5. Zero Tolerance Is a Harmful School Policy for Teens   **168**
  Annette Fuentes

Periodical and Internet Sources Bibliography   **175**

For Further Discussion   **176**

Organizations to Contact   **179**

Bibliography of Books   **186**

Index   **190**

Why Consider Opposing Viewpoints?

> *"The only way in which a human being can make some approach to knowing the whole of a subject is by hearing what can be said about it by persons of every variety of opinion and studying all modes in which it can be looked at by every character of mind. No wise man ever acquired his wisdom in any mode but this."*
>
> *John Stuart Mill*

In our media-intensive culture it is not difficult to find differing opinions. Thousands of newspapers and magazines and dozens of radio and television talk shows resound with differing points of view. The difficulty lies in deciding which opinion to agree with and which "experts" seem the most credible. The more inundated we become with differing opinions and claims, the more essential it is to hone critical reading and thinking skills to evaluate these ideas. Opposing Viewpoints books address this problem directly by presenting stimulating debates that can be used to enhance and teach these skills. The varied opinions contained in each book examine many different aspects of a single issue. While examining these conveniently edited opposing views, readers can develop critical thinking skills such as the ability to compare and contrast authors' credibility, facts, argumentation styles, use of persuasive techniques, and other stylistic tools. In short, the Opposing Viewpoints Series is an ideal way to attain the higher-level thinking and reading skills so essential in a culture of diverse and contradictory opinions.

In addition to providing a tool for critical thinking, Opposing Viewpoints books challenge readers to question their own strongly held opinions and assumptions. Most people form their opinions on the basis of upbringing, peer pressure, and personal, cultural, or professional bias. By reading carefully balanced opposing views, readers must directly confront new ideas as well as the opinions of those with whom they disagree. This is not to argue simplistically that everyone who reads opposing views will—or should—change his or her opinion. Instead, the series enhances readers' understanding of their own views by encouraging confrontation with opposing ideas. Careful examination of others' views can lead to the readers' understanding of the logical inconsistencies in their own opinions, perspective on why they hold an opinion, and the consideration of the possibility that their opinion requires further evaluation.

Evaluating Other Opinions

To ensure that this type of examination occurs, Opposing Viewpoints books present all types of opinions. Prominent spokespeople on different sides of each issue as well as well-known professionals from many disciplines challenge the reader. An additional goal of the series is to provide a forum for other, less known, or even unpopular viewpoints. The opinion of an ordinary person who has had to make the decision to cut off life support from a terminally ill relative, for example, may be just as valuable and provide just as much insight as a medical ethicist's professional opinion. The editors have two additional purposes in including these less known views. One, the editors encourage readers to respect others' opinions—even when not enhanced by professional credibility. It is only by reading or listening to and objectively evaluating others' ideas that one can determine whether they are worthy of consideration. Two, the inclusion of such viewpoints encourages the important critical thinking skill of objectively evaluating an author's credentials and bias. This evaluation will illuminate an author's reasons for taking a particular stance on an issue and will aid in readers' evaluation of the author's ideas.

It is our hope that these books will give readers a deeper understanding of the issues debated and an appreciation of the complexity of even seemingly simple issues when good and honest people disagree. This awareness is particularly important in a democratic society such as ours in which people enter into public debate to determine the common good. Those with whom one disagrees should not be regarded as enemies but rather as people whose views deserve careful examination and may shed light on one's own.

Thomas Jefferson once said that "difference of opinion leads to inquiry, and inquiry to truth." Jefferson, a broadly educated man, argued that "if a nation expects to be ignorant and free . . . it expects what never was and never will be." As individuals and as a nation, it is imperative that we consider the opinions of others and examine them with skill and discernment. The Opposing Viewpoints Series is intended to help readers achieve this goal.

David L. Bender and Bruno Leone,
Founders

Introduction

"Digital technology has fabulously empowered [young people]. . . . Yet adolescents use these tools to wrap themselves in a generational cocoon filled with puerile banter and coarse images."

> Mark Bauerlein, author of
> The Dumbest Generation: How
> the Digital Age Stupefies Young
> Americans and Jeopardizes
> Our Future

"Although this digital immersion presents significant challenges for young people . . . their immersion has not hurt them at all. It has been positive."

> Don Tapscott, expert on digital
> technology and author of Grown
> Up Digital: How the Net
> Generation is Changing
> Your World

Americans born during the last twenty years live in a substantially different world than their parents. The rise of the Internet, social media networks, and video games has created what many are calling a "digital divide" between teens and their parents. Some are even calling the current wave of teenagers the "digital generation." While it is difficult to pin a label on any large group of people, most observers agree that, through technology, teenagers today are connected to each other and their world in more intricate ways than any generation of teens before them.

Of course, teens are still faced with the same problems as their predecessors, but they now have a new set of problems related to digital technology and freedoms that put them at risk in new and unforeseen ways.

As much as access to the Internet has improved the lives of teens, it has also been a source of new problems. For example, while parents debate the relative merits of comprehensive sex education versus abstinence-only sex education, a high percentage of young people get their first exposure to sex through online pornography. In his book *Forbidden Fruit: Sex & Religion in the Lives of American Teenagers*, Mark D. Regnerus argues that "unless this digital revolution in sexual education and socialization is recognized and contested—and soon—the school sex education instructor will become, as Pink Floyd put it, 'just another brick in the wall.'" Online pornography promotes neither abstinence nor "protected" safe sex practices, nor does it educate in any way about the emotional component of sexuality.

The freedom to experiment and quickly share information with new technology has also given rise to problems. Some teens have engaged in "sexting" in which sexually provocative photos are sent to others, with a range of ramifications from pure mortification to criminal charges. The ability to share personal information and thoughts freely can lead to increased friendships as well as misunderstandings, sexual harassment, and bullying.

Video games—including online multiplayer gaming—have also introduced new risks. It is estimated that teens spend approximately three to four times more hours involved with games and social media than on homework. Books with titles such as *The Dumbest Generation: How the Digital Age Stupefies Young Americans and Jeopardizes Our Future* by Mark Bauerlein lament this trend. Other books, such as *Reality Is Broken: Why Games Make Us Better and How They Can Change the World* by Jane McGonigal, are highly optimistic about digital technology and its potential applications in the realm of education. While the debate continues about the overall effects of digital technology, experts *do* agree that gaming and social media are contributing factors in the recent decline in physical activity and related increase in teenage obesity.

Teenage use of the Internet, social media, and gaming has direct ramifications for teen education and an impact on problems such as obesity, bullying, and suicide. The authors in *Opposing Viewpoints: Teens at Risk* explore these issues in the following chapters: What Factors Put Teens at Risk?, How Does Substance Abuse Impact Teens?, Does Sexuality Put Teens at Risk?, and How Should Society Deal with Teen Discipline and Teen Crime? Though many of the issues facing teens are the same ones their parents faced, there are new risks for teens today, including some that are exacerbated by digital technology.

CHAPTER 1

What Factors Put Teens at Risk?

Chapter Preface

Many powerful external forces put teens at risk. The wide-spread availability of illegal drugs and alcohol, the in-your-face sexual messages of popular music and movies, the uncensored freedom of information on the Internet, poverty and chronic unemployment, the inability of high schools and colleges to retain and successfully educate a majority of young people—all these forces play a role in putting teens at risk. Recent studies of the teenage brain have shown that internal stresses and brain developments also lead teens to willingly put themselves at risk. As scholar Sheryl Feinstein notes in her book *Inside the Teenage Brain*:

> The teenage propensity to take risks comes from a variety of sources, including trying to impress peers, an indestructible belief about themselves, and the changes in their brains. Novelty and danger are a tantalizing combination. They stimulate dopamine production, and in combination, create the same rush that drugs like crack and meth generate.

In their quest for new experiences and a sense of identity, teens try many activities that adults perceive as reckless. Many of these behaviors can be seen as a reaction to the stresses felt by teens today.

Many teens today feel isolated from society and that they have little control over the larger forces that influence their lives. This generation of teens grew up in the context of the Columbine High School massacre (1999), 9/11 (2001), and the Virginia Tech massacre (2007). In a 2010 survey of teen attitudes by MTV and the Associated Press, 38 percent of teens complain of frequently feeling stress and anxiety. In contrast, other recent surveys of teen satisfaction, including one by Students Against Destructive Decisions (SADD), have shown that the vast majority of teens (about three of four) feel "happy" most days and have a strongly positive view of themselves and their future. But perhaps there is no real contradiction between teens who feel generally happy and yet also feel frequently stressed. In any case, as psychologists Joseph Allen and Claudia Worrell Allen have observed, the majority of teens today feel as if they live in an unreal "bubble" that has little connection to the outside world. One dimension of that bubble is the high school institution.

Teens feel enormous pressure as they seek to navigate the complex, sometimes arcane world of high school with its myriad rules, both academic and social, that are written and unwritten. The MTV and AP survey found that teens see school as the biggest source of stress in their lives. Parental expectations about school achievement tend to be higher than for previous generations, and participation in extracurricular activities and school sports is at an all time high. The number of students taking Advanced Placement classes has doubled over the last ten years. In addition, many teens face parental and peer pressure to make good grades to prepare for the competitive college admissions process. These pressures tend to make teens doubt themselves and feel bad when they don't meet the high expectations placed upon them. One response to these feelings is to do what they know will make them feel better—have fun with their friends. This may include escaping into video games, social networks, or browsing the Internet. It may or may not involve the use of substances such as beer and marijuana to relieve stress. The desire to relieve the stresses of being a teenager may also lead to overeating or extreme behaviors such as cutting, eating disorders, or even suicide. These and other factors that put teens at risk are examined in the following chapter.

> *"We're so used to seeing adolescence as a problem. But the more we learn . . . the more adolescence starts to seem like a highly functional, even adaptive period."*

Risk Taking Is a Positive Function of the Teenage Brain

David Dobbs

In the following viewpoint, David Dobbs explores recent scientific studies about the teenage brain. In contrast to the popular view that teen behavior is largely dysfunctional or unproductive, new scientific studies suggest that late adolescence is when the brain matures significantly, preparing teens to adapt to the outside world. In this view, even thrill-seeking and risk-taking behaviors serve a positive evolutionary function for teens. Dobbs is the author of numerous articles and books about science and culture.

As you read, consider the following questions:

1. According to the author, how did scientists first discover that the teenage brain is still going through enormous changes?

David Dobbs, "The New Science of the Teenage Brain," *National Geographic*, vol. 218, no. 4, October 2011, pp. 42–43, 48–49, 54–55, 59. Copyright © 2011 by National Geographic Society. All rights reserved. Reproduced by permission.

2. Even though teens recognize risk as well as adults, according to the viewpoint, why do they take more dangerous chances?

3. The author suggests that socializing intensely with peers, taking risks, and other late adolescent traits are all necessary preparation for what vitally important moment for teens?

One fine May morning not long ago my oldest son, 17 at the time, phoned to tell me that he had just spent a couple hours at the state police barracks. Apparently he had been driving "a little fast." What, I asked, was "a little fast"? Turns out this product of my genes and loving care, the boy-man I had swaddled, coddled, cooed at, and then pushed and pulled to the brink of manhood, had been flying down the highway at 113 miles an hour.

"That's more than a little fast," I said.

He agreed. In fact, he sounded somber and contrite. He did not object when I told him he'd have to pay the fines and probably for a lawyer. He did not argue when I pointed out that if anything happens at that speed—a dog in the road, a blown tire, a sneeze—he dies. He was in fact almost irritatingly reasonable. He even proffered that the cop did the right thing in stopping him, for, as he put it, "We can't all go around doing 113."

He did, however, object to one thing. He didn't like it that one of the several citations he received was for reckless driving.

"Well," I huffed, sensing an opportunity to finally yell at him, "what would you call it?"

"It's just not accurate," he said calmly. "'Reckless' sounds like you're not paying attention. But I was. I made a deliberate point of doing this on an empty stretch of dry interstate, in broad daylight, with good sight lines and no traffic. I mean, I wasn't just gunning the thing. I was driving.

"I guess that's what I want you to know. If it makes you feel any better, I was really focused."

Actually, it did make me feel better. That bothered me, for I didn't understand why. Now I do.

The Mystery of Teen Behavior

My son's high-speed adventure raised the question long asked by people who have pondered the class of humans we call teenagers: What on Earth was he doing? Parents often phrase this question more colorfully. Scientists put it more coolly. They ask, What can explain this behavior? But even that is just another way of wondering, What is wrong with these kids? Why do they act this way? The question passes judgment even as it inquires.

Through the ages, most answers have cited dark forces that uniquely affect the teen. Aristotle concluded more than 2,300 years ago that "the young are heated by Nature as drunken men by wine." A shepherd in William Shakespeare's *The Winter's Tale* wishes "there were no age between ten and three-and-twenty, or that youth would sleep out the rest; for there is nothing in the between but getting wenches with child, wronging the ancientry, stealing, fighting." His lament colors most modern scientific inquiries as well. . . . [Sigmund] Freud saw adolescence as an expression of torturous psychosexual conflict; [psychologist] Erik Erikson, as the most tumultuous of life's several identity crises. Adolescence: always a problem.

Such thinking carried into the late 20th century, when researchers developed brain-imaging technology that enabled them to see the teen brain in enough detail to track both its physical development and its patterns of activity. These imaging tools offered a new way to ask the same question—What's wrong with these kids?—and revealed an answer that surprised almost everyone. Our brains, it turned out, take much longer to develop than we had thought. This revelation suggested both a simplistic, unflattering explanation for teens' maddening behavior—and a more complex, affirmative explanation as well.

Teens Undergo Brain Reorganization

The first full series of scans of the developing adolescent brain—a National Institutes of Health (NIH) project that studied over a hundred young people as they grew up during the 1990s—showed that our brains undergo a massive reorganization between our 12th and 25th years. The brain doesn't actually grow very much during this period. It has already reached 90 percent of its full size by the time a person is six, and a thickening skull accounts for most head growth afterward. But as we move through adolescence, the brain undergoes extensive remodeling, resembling a network and wiring upgrade. . . .

This process of maturation, once thought to be largely finished by elementary school, continues throughout adolescence. Imaging work done since the 1990s shows that these physical changes move in a slow wave from the brain's rear to its front, from areas close to the brain stem that look after older and more behaviorally basic functions, such as vision, movement, and fundamental processing, to the evolutionarily newer and more complicated thinking areas up front. The corpus callosum, which connects the brain's left and right hemispheres and carries traffic essential to many advanced brain functions, steadily thickens. Stronger links also develop between the hippocampus, a sort of memory directory, and frontal areas that set goals and weigh different agendas; as a result, we get better at integrating memory and experience into our decisions. At the same time, the frontal areas develop greater speed and richer connections, allowing us to generate and weigh far more variables and agendas than before.

When this development proceeds normally, we get better at balancing impulse, desire, goals, self-interest, rules, ethics, and even altruism, generating behavior that is more complex and, sometimes at least, more sensible. But at times, and especially at first, the brain does this work clumsily. It's hard to get all those new cogs to mesh. . . .

Teens Are Learning to Use a New Network

These studies help explain why teens behave with such vexing inconsistency: beguiling at breakfast, disgusting at dinner; masterful on Monday, sleepwalking on Saturday. Along with lacking experience generally, they're still learning to use their brain's new networks. Stress, fatigue, or challenges can cause a misfire. Abigail Baird, a Vassar psychologist who studies teens, calls this neural gawkiness—an equivalent to the physical awkwardness teens sometimes display while mastering their growing bodies.

The slow and uneven developmental arc revealed by these imaging studies offers an alluringly pithy explanation for why teens may do stupid things like drive at 113 miles an hour, aggrieve their ancientry, and get people (or get gotten) with child: They act that way because their brains aren't done! You can see it right there in the scans!

This view, as titles from the explosion of scientific papers and popular articles about the "teen brain" put it, presents adolescents as "works in progress" whose "immature brains" lead some to question whether they are in a state "akin to mental retardation."

The story you're reading right now, however, tells a different scientific tale about the teen brain. Over the past five years or so, even as the work-in-progress story spread into our culture, the discipline of adolescent brain studies learned to do some more-complex thinking of its own. A few researchers began to view recent brain and genetic findings in a brighter, more flattering light, one distinctly colored by evolutionary theory. The resulting account of the adolescent brain—call it the adaptive-adolescent story—casts the teen less as a rough draft than as an exquisitely sensitive, highly adaptable creature wired almost perfectly for the job of moving from the safety of home into the complicated world outside.

The Brain Is Adaptive

This view will likely sit better with teens. More important, it sits better with biology's most fundamental principle, that of natural selection. Selection is hell on dysfunctional traits. If adolescence is essentially a collection of them—angst, idiocy, and haste; impulsiveness, selfishness, and reckless bumbling— then how did those traits survive selection? They couldn't—not if they were the period's most fundamental or consequential features.

The answer is that those troublesome traits don't really characterize adolescence; they're just what we notice most because they annoy us or put our children in danger. As B.J. Casey, a neuroscientist at Weill Cornell Medical College who has spent nearly a decade applying brain and genetic studies to our understanding of adolescence, puts it, "We're so used to seeing adolescence as a problem. But the more we learn about what really makes this period unique, the more adolescence starts to seem like a highly functional, even adaptive period. It's exactly what you'd need to do the things you have to do then."

To see past the distracting, dopey teenager and glimpse the adaptive adolescent within, we should look not at specific, sometimes startling, behaviors, such as skateboarding down stairways or dating fast company, but at the broader traits that underlie those acts.

Sensation Seeking Is at Its Peak

Let's start with the teen's love of the thrill. We all like new and exciting things, but we never value them more highly than we do during adolescence. Here we hit a high in what behavioral scientists call sensation seeking: the hunt for the neural buzz, the jolt of the unusual or unexpected.

Seeking sensation isn't necessarily impulsive. You might plan a sensation-seeking experience—a skydive or a fast drive—quite deliberately, as my son did. Impulsivity generally drops throughout life, starting at about age 10, but this love of the thrill peaks at around age 15. And although sensation seeking can lead to dangerous behaviors, it can also generate positive ones: The urge to meet more people, for instance, can create a wider circle of friends, which generally makes us healthier, happier, safer, and more successful.

This upside probably explains why an openness to the new, though it can sometimes kill the cat, remains a highlight of adolescent development. A love of novelty leads directly to useful experience. More broadly, the hunt for sensation provides the inspiration needed to "get you out of the house" and into new terrain, as Jay Giedd, a pioneering researcher in teen brain development at NIH [National Institute of Health], puts it.

Risk-Taking Is at Its Peak

Also peaking during adolescence (and perhaps aggrieving the ancientry the most) is risk-taking. We court risk more avidly as teens than at any other time. This shows reliably in the lab, where teens take more chances in controlled experiments involving everything from card games to simulated driving. And it shows in real life, where the period from roughly 15 to 25 brings peaks in all sorts of risky ventures and ugly outcomes. This age group dies of accidents of almost every sort (other than work accidents) at high rates. Most long-term drug or alcohol abuse starts during adolescence, and even people who later drink responsibly often drink too much as teens. Especially in cultures where teenage driving is common, this takes a gory toll: In the U.S., one in three teen deaths is from car crashes, many involving alcohol.

Are these kids just being stupid? That's the conventional explanation: They're not thinking, or by the work-in-progress model, their puny developing brains fail them.

Yet these explanations don't hold up. As Laurence Steinberg, a developmental psychologist specializing in adolescence at Temple University, points out, even 14- to 17-year-olds—the biggest risktakers—use the same basic cognitive strategies that adults do, and they usually reason their way through problems just as well as adults. Contrary to popular belief, they also fully recognize they're mortal. And, like adults, says Steinberg, "teens actually overestimate risk."

How Teens Weigh Risk vs. Reward

So if teens think as well as adults do and recognize risk just as well, why do they take more chances? Here, as elsewhere, the problem lies less in what teens lack compared with adults than in what they have more of. Teens take more risks not because they don't understand the dangers but because they weigh risk versus reward differently. In situations where risk can get them something they want, they value the reward more heavily than adults do. . . .

Researchers such as Steinberg and Casey believe this risk-friendly weighing of cost versus reward has been selected for because, over the course of human evolution, the willingness to take risks during this period of life has granted an adaptive edge. Succeeding often requires moving out of the home and into less secure situations. "The more you seek novelty and take risks," says Baird, "the better you do." This responsiveness to reward thus works like the desire for new sensation: It gets you out of the house and into new turf. . . .

The teen brain is similarly attuned to oxytocin, another neural hormone, which (among other things) makes social connections in particular more rewarding. The neural networks and dynamics associated with general reward and social interactions overlap heavily. Engage one, and you often engage the other. Engage them during adolescence, and you light a fire.

The Pull of the Social Scene

This helps explain another trait that marks adolescence: Teens prefer the company of those their own age more than ever before or after. At one level, this passion for same-age peers merely expresses in the social realm the teen's general attraction to novelty: Teens offer teens far more novelty than familiar old family does.

Yet teens gravitate toward peers for another, more powerful reason: to invest in the future rather than the past. We enter a world made by our parents. But we will live most of our lives, and prosper (or not) in a world run and remade by our peers. Knowing, understanding, and building relationships with them bears critically on success. Socially savvy rats or monkeys, for instance, generally get the best nesting areas or territories, the most food and water, more allies, and more sex with better and fitter mates. And no species is more intricately and deeply social than humans are.

This supremely human characteristic makes peer relations not a sideshow but the main show. Some brain-scan studies, in fact, suggest that our brains react to peer exclusion much as they respond to threats to physical health or food supply. At a neural level, in other words, we perceive social rejection as a threat to existence. Knowing this might make it easier to abide the hysteria of a 13-year-old deceived by a friend or the gloom of a 15-year-old not invited to a party. These people! we lament. They react to social ups and downs as if their fates depended upon them! They're right. They do.

The Move Away from Home

Excitement, novelty, risk, the company of peers. These traits may seem to add up to nothing more than doing foolish new stuff with friends. Look deeper, however, and you see that these traits that define adolescence make us more adaptive, both as individuals and as a species. . . .

Culture clearly shapes adolescence. It influences its expression and possibly its length. It can magnify its manifestations. Yet culture does not create adolescence. The period's uniqueness rises from genes and developmental processes that have been selected for over thousands of generations because they play an amplified role during this key transitional period: producing a creature optimally primed to leave a safe home and move into unfamiliar territory.

The move outward from home is the most difficult thing that humans do, as well as the most critical—not just for individuals but for a species that has shown an unmatched ability to master challenging new environments. In scientific terms, teenagers can be a pain in the ass. But they are quite possibly the most fully, crucially adaptive human beings around. Without them, humanity might not have so readily spread across the globe.

> "When I see a kid who is overweight,
> knowing that . . . [this] could lead
> to life-long health problems . . . I feel
> that parents and society are not doing
> their job."

Teen Food Options Promote Obesity and Poor Health

Eric A. Finkelstein and Laurie Zuckerman

Eric A. Finkelstein and Laurie Zuckerman observe in the following viewpoint that the percentage of overweight teens has tripled in the past thirty years. The consequences of this include discrimination, low self-esteem, and a much higher risk for life-shortening diseases. The authors contend that the primary blame for this lies with those who make the most food and health decisions for children: parents and educators. Finkelstein is a professor at Duke University and a nationally recognized expert on economics and obesity; Zuckerman is a writer on health care, high tech, and business.

As you read, consider the following questions:

1. In recent years, which disease associated with obesity has doubled among children, according to the viewpoint?
2. According to one study cited in the viewpoint, what is the relationship between obesity and girls' puberty?

3. What percent of high schools make junk food available through vending machines or stores, according to the authors?

Currently, about 17 percent of U.S. children are overweight, and many more are at risk of becoming overweight, based on the government's definition of excess weight among youth. *Overweight* is the government's polite term for obese kids, and *at-risk* is their terminology for overweight kids.

As an aside, if you find these terms misleading, you are not alone. Recently, an expert panel made up of members of the American Medical Association and the Centers for Disease Control and Prevention (CDC) met to discuss a change in terminology. They claimed that these terms did not adequately represent the weight problem facing America's youth. . . .

A Rising Number of Overweight Youth

Regardless of terminology, even more alarming than the high prevalence is the rate at which excess weight is rising among America's youth. Government data reveals that the rate of overweight 6 to 11 year olds tripled from 4 percent to almost 19 percent during the past 30 years. The rate for 12 to 19 year olds mirrored that jump, with an increase in prevalence from 6 percent to over 17 percent. Even preschoolers are putting on the pounds. Since 1990, twice as many children between the ages of 2 and 5 are overweight (13.9 percent compared to 7.2 percent).

Though children of all ethnic groups have gained weight, certain racial, ethnic, and socioeconomic groups have put on the most. As was the case 30 years ago, excess weight remains more common among African-American and Hispanic children than among whites. Whereas the gap between ethnic groups is shrinking for adults, it is growing for kids. According to a national study, from 1986 to 1998, overweight prevalence rose by more than 120 percent among African-American and Hispanic children compared with 50 percent among Caucasians.

So what are the consequences for these kids? Sadly, given so-cietal norms that reward thinness, these kids are likely to face significant discrimination throughout their lives. Moreover, dis-crimination and prejudice can begin at a very young age. Studies on children as young as five years old show that they have already absorbed our cultural bias against fat.

The Link Between Obesity and Discrimination

Being the target of prejudice can be devastating for overweight children. They are more likely to be sad, lonely, and nervous. One study shocked even a jaded obesity researcher like me: The study found that children who were overweight rated their qual-ity of life as being similar to children who were being treated for cancer. Talk about a sobering comparison!

And the effects can stick around. Being overweight during childhood can have lasting effects on self-esteem, body image, and economic mobility. Overweight children sometimes per-ceive themselves as unattractive, which may lead to depression, disordered eating, and risky behaviors such as tobacco and alco-hol abuse.

Even parents have been known to discriminate against their own overweight children. One study showed that parents of over-weight daughters will not spend as much money on their daugh-ters' college education as parents of normal-weight daughters.

If the social impact is heartbreaking, the health prognosis for these children is equally disturbing. . . .

Obesity Can Lead to a Decline in Life Expectancy

Well, researchers at the University of Illinois at Chicago have made a surprising new prediction: Due to increases in the preva-lence of childhood obesity, today's children may not live as long as their parents. The study suggests that weight problems could cancel out life-extending benefits of medical advances in the

"'Not a significant source of anything even remotely nutritious' . . . Wow, Mom, can we get these?," cartoon by Brian Fray. www.CartoonStock.com.

coming decades. As a direct result, the United States could be facing its first sustained drop in life expectancy in the modern era.

"It's one thing for an adult of 45 or 55 to develop type 2 diabetes and then experience the life-threatening complications of that—kidney failure, heart attack, stroke—in their late 50s or 60s," said Dr. David Ludwig. "But for a 4-year-old or 6-year-old who's obese to develop type 2 diabetes at 14 or 16 raises the possibility of devastating complications before reaching age 30. It's really a staggering prospect."

Indeed, children are increasingly showing up in pediatricians' offices with type 2 diabetes and other conditions once known only to adults (type 2 diabetes was once synonymous with adult-onset diabetes, but thanks to the rise in childhood obesity and the prevalence of this condition in overweight kids, that is no longer the case). The American Diabetes Association now estimates that as many as 45 percent of new cases of pediatric diabetes may be type 2 (not the more common type 1, or juvenile diabetes). In fact, one study found that the number of type 2 diabetes prescriptions among children doubled from 2002 to 2005.

Obesity Results in Higher Risk of Disease

Excess weight during childhood can also significantly increase the risk of disease and obesity in adulthood. Cardiovascular risk factors, for example, can be carried from childhood into adulthood, which predispose adults to severe chronic conditions such as heart failure.

A recent study reported that increasing rates of childhood obesity also appear to be causing girls to reach puberty at an earlier age. Results showed that the mean age of onset of breast development, which had been close to 11 years in earlier studies, is now approximately 10 years in Caucasian girls and just under nine years in African-American girls. The study's author reported: "Earlier onset of puberty in girls has been associated with a number of adverse outcomes, including psychiatric disorders and deficits in psychosocial functioning, earlier initiation of alcohol use, sexual intercourse and teenage pregnancy and increased rates of adult obesity and reproductive cancers."

So this is the kind of bleak information I encounter every day. And, yes, it bothers me. . . . While adults have the ability to make informed choices related to diet, exercise, and weight, children do not. Most of their food consumption and physical activity decisions are made for them by parents or school administrators. So when I see a kid who is overweight, knowing that his or her excess weight will be very difficult to reverse later in life and could lead to life-long health problems and a shorter life expectancy, I feel that parents and society are not doing their job. . . .

The Increase in Caloric Consumption

Since the late 1970s, children have increased their caloric consumption as well. Adolescent boys now average about 2,800 calories a day, an increase of 250 calories. Similarly, adolescent girls now average approximately 1,900 calories, an increase of 120 calories. (In comparison, adult men have increased their daily food intake by about 180 calories, and women have increased their daily food intake by about 360 calories.)

Children between the ages of 6 and 11 consume 21 to 23 teaspoons of added sugars per day, far surpassing the government recommendations of 6 to 12. They also eat three times as many chips/crackers/popcorn/pretzels as they did in the mid-1970s. Adolescent boys now consume 22 ounces of soft drinks a day, up from 7 ounces in the 1970s. If none of these additional 15 ounces are diet soft drinks, this increase represents approximately 250 additional calories.

So what's behind the increased caloric intake for kids? All of the obesity-inducing factors . . . [such as] the cheap supersized meals, the diet becoming richer in fats and sugars, the snacking, the meals out—are still relevant, but there is one other often-cited culprit in the picture: our public schools.

The Problem with School Foods

Although the picture is beginning to change, schools have traditionally not been a beacon of healthy eating. A recent study has shown that children who eat school lunches consume 40 to 120 more calories as a result of this meal compared to children who bring their lunch from home.

Then there are vending machines and snack foods—a hard-to-resist revenue stream for schools struggling to get by with significant state budget shortfalls. Some have even entered exclusive and highly controversial "pouring rights" agreements with soda manufacturers in order to create more discretionary funds. Typically, these contracts require the schools to promise to sell a certain number of sodas a year, a relationship that opponents say transforms the school's role from being a provider of vending machines to being an active soda peddler.

And the picture just gets worse as kids get older. Availability of junk food increases with grade level—in 2000, 43 percent of elementary schools, 89 percent of middle schools, and 98 percent of high schools had student-accessible vending machines or stores where junk foods could be purchased.

"Gamers often find themselves lost in an online fantasy world, while compulsive users of social networking sites lose themselves in online fantasy relationships."

Cyber Junkie: Escape the Gaming and Internet Trap

Kevin Roberts

In the following viewpoint, Kevin Roberts describes the cases of several boys he worked with who exhibited classic signs of video game addiction—where the desire to play video games overpowered all other interests. Roberts describes the warning signs of video game addiction and some of the practical steps needed to combat the problem. Roberts, a recovering video game and social networking addict, is the author of Cyber Junkie: Escape the Gaming and Internet Trap.

As you read, consider the following questions:

1. According to the author, what is frequently the first warning sign of video game addiction?
2. Name one of the highly addictive games that uses clans or guilds, as noted in the viewpoint.

3. Most cyber addicts, in the author's experience, have difficulties in what aspect of their lives?

Sleepless Nights, Bad Grades

A 2009 study showed a strong correlation between excessive daytime sleepiness and extreme Internet use in adolescents. Correlations with a variety of other sleep problems were also observed. When adolescents exhibit low mental energy and are continually fatigued, Internet use should be one of the first variables examined. Sleep disturbances are often the first sign of a cyber problem. Since the brain does not function well on short sleep, problems in school, therefore, are usually not far behind.

Connor was seventeen and performing poorly in school when he came to see me in my role as an academic/learning coach. He had an IQ of 135 but suffered from ADHD. He was a math whiz who did well in calculus without really studying, but his grades in other subjects left much to be desired. He was tired all the time and frequently fell asleep during class. Connor told his mother that he had been going to bed around eleven and waking up around seven.

Eager to solve the mystery of his tiredness, Connor's mother took him to a sleep clinic. The doctors found nothing wrong. I suspected video games, but his mother did not agree. She knew he liked computer games but had never seen him playing for long periods. His sleepiness seemed to be the key to his low grades, but we did not know what was keeping him awake at night.

We were at an impasse until another boy who was a client of mine and knew Connor from school told me that Connor stayed up all night playing *World of Warcraft*. Connor had bragged about his online exploits on his Facebook page. When I confronted him, he admitted that this was true. It took many attempts over several weeks, however, to convince him that spending his nights on the game and not sleeping underlay his lack of academic success and constant irritability. He wanted to do well in school, cared about his grades, and he really wanted to stop gaming.

Many discussions over those several weeks culminated in Connor finally committing to face his problem. He seemed to turn over a new leaf. He brought me his copy of the game in a sort of ritual to symbolize his commitment to recovery. He actually started sleeping, and teachers began to email his mother favorable reports. It was a swift and miraculous turnaround.

He phoned me whenever he felt a relapse coming on. "Kevin, it's Connor," he'd anxiously say. "I got a new copy of the game from a friend, and I'm really close to putting it back on the computer." I talked him through it and together we figured out solutions when the cravings were intense.

I had been receiving this sort of phone call from him regularly for a couple months, and then they abruptly stopped. I naively figured the cravings had subsided. But a couple of weeks later, Connor was tired and irritable again. He would not admit to backsliding, but that same week his mother caught him playing *World of Warcraft* at five in the morning.

Despite Connor's desperate desire to do well in school, the need to play the game overpowered the desire for good grades. Out of desperation, his parents sent him to a therapeutic wilderness school far away from his electronic universe. Connor is thriving in that environment, but the real test will come when he returns home and has to deal with temptation. . . .

In the Shadows

Cyber junkies steal away to secret locations to peacefully pursue cyber pleasure away from prying eyes and inquisitive minds. We often interface with our fantasy realms in places and at times that minimize contact with the outside world. "My son is a virtual night owl," one mother told me, "and I'm not sure he ever sleeps. If I wake up at four in the morning, he's on that stupid game." A loved one gaming in the middle of the night is often the first sign of a problem.

Video Game Addiction

Gaming becomes a habit that some kids can't kick. When your son plays an exciting or violent video game, his heart rate increases, his breathing quickens, and his blood pressure goes up. In some cases, particularly when games offer surprising or disturbing scenarios, players' brains release the hormone cortisol, making it more likely that the players will remember what they've seen or heard.

For some people, the physical changes the body undergoes during the playing of video games can lead to full-blown addiction. In 1998, a group of researchers in Britain using positron-emission tomography (PET) scans identified the neurochemical foundation of what can become a debilitating and uncontrollable compulsion to game. They charted the brain chemistry of gamers as they maneuvered convoys through a battlefield and destroyed enemy tanks. The scientists found that the brains of these players released massive amounts of dopamine. This is the same neurochemical response that occurs in the brains of cocaine addicts when they snort their drug of choice. Just like classic addicts, problem video gamers develop "triggers" that lead them to play more and more.

Peg Tyre, The Trouble with Boys. *New York: Crown Publishers, 2008, p. 190.*

Like most addicts, we hide our behavior. Openly displaying our tendency to excessively game or obsess over our social networking site profiles has resulted in scolding and criticism. If we live at home with our parents, we are more than happy to have our bedroom in the basement. If we live in a house, with others, whether family or friends, we consider our bedroom a holy place. We deem it an extreme sign of disrespect for you to enter without permission. We do not want you in there at all. We want to be alone and uninterrupted while indulging in our obsession. Our dream is our own secluded cyber lair.

The game console and the social network interface are portals to another world. When you talk to us or the phone rings, we are forced to come back to the real world. We find that irritating. We neither desire to see your face nor hear your voice when we are in that virtual space. From our perspective, any interruption is an extreme violation. We want you to stay away. . . .

Spend Time with Friends or Go Online?

Those who have a cyber addict in their lives commonly feel neglected and unimportant, just as they would with any other addict. In the throes of a binge, I have turned off my phone, shut all the shades, and reacted viciously when interrupted. I did not want my union with my game or the cyber world interrupted. In those moments, I was escaping the real world, and I resented anyone who tried to bring me back. "Leave me alone!"

Most cyber addicts who come to see me, whether child or adult, experience difficulties in relationships. Sometimes those difficulties are a direct result of the compulsive cyber use, but other times existing social problems are what propel users into an alternate reality. Gamers often find themselves lost in an online fantasy world, while compulsive users of social networking sites lose themselves in online fantasy relationships. They interact through a screen for seven, eight, or even ten hours a day. Gamers join clans and guilds in games such as *World of Warcraft*, *EverQuest*, *RuneScape*, and *Counter-Strike*. They spend little time with their friends or spouses, and rush home from school or work to log on to the game so that they can support their clan. Those with social networking addictions won't be bothered to call or meet with friends, but they obsess over their MySpace and Facebook profile pages as if they were primping for a date.

The consequences for the addict, whether adolescent or adult, are severe as use spirals out of control. The addict may even fail to perform the most basic responsibilities as he or she loses a grasp on reality. . . .

With all addictions, the addictive activity or substance dwarfs all other activities and the people from whom the addict once derived pleasure and sustenance. The extent to which an addict ignores loved ones is a useful measure in determining the depth of the addiction.

| "There are reasons to believe that violent video games may have a larger harmful effect than violent TV and film."

Violent Video Games Promote Teen Aggression and Violence

Craig A. Anderson

In the following viewpoint, Craig A. Anderson discusses the influence of media violence—including violent video games—on youth. Anderson contends that the research demonstrates a clear connection between violent video games and teen aggression. Anderson is a professor at Iowa State University and one of the leading experts about studies on media violence.

As you read, consider the following questions:

1. The viewpoint notes a distinction between violence depicted in passive forms and active forms of media. What is one of the passive forms of media?
2. According to the author, is there a direct link between use of violent video games and the well-known incidents of school shootings?

3. Why, according to the viewpoint, does the entertainment industry spend so much money arguing against the connection between media violence and aggression?

1. *For your 2003 article on* The Influence of Media Violence on Youth, *you and a distinguished group of media scholars selected by the National Institute of Mental Health reviewed 50 years of research on media violence and aggression. What have been the main research steps, and what are the main conclusions?*

Craig A. Anderson: Most of the early research focused on two questions:

1. Is there a significant association between exposure to media violence and aggressive behavior?
2. Is this association causal? (That is, can we say that violent television, video games, and other media are directly causing aggressive behavior in our kids?)

Media Violence Causes Aggressive Behavior

The results, overall, have been fairly consistent across types of studies (experimental, cross-sectional, and longitudinal) and across visual media type (television, films, video games). There is a significant relation between exposure to media violence and aggressive behavior. Exposing children and adolescents (or "youth") to violent visual media increases the likelihood that they will engage in physical aggression against another person. By "physical aggression" we mean behavior that is intended to harm another person physically, such as hitting with a fist or some object. A single brief exposure to violent media can increase aggression in the immediate situation. Repeated exposure leads to general increases in aggressiveness over time. This relation between media violence and aggressive behavior is causal.

2. What have researchers focused on in more recent years? How does exposure to media violence increase later aggressive behavior?

Early aggression researchers were interested in discovering how youth learn to be aggressive. Once they discovered observational learning takes place not only when youth see how people behave in the real world but also when they see characters in films and on television, many began to focus on exactly how watching such violent stories increases later aggression. In other words, more recent research really focused on the underlying psychological mechanisms. In the last 10 years there also has been a huge increase in research on violent video games. Based on five decades of research on television and film violence and one decade of research on video games, we now have a pretty clear picture of how exposure to media violence can increase aggression in both the immediate situation as well as in long term contexts.

The Short-Term Impact of Media Violence

Immediately after consuming some media violence, there is an increase in aggressive behavior tendencies because of several factors.

1. Aggressive thoughts increase, which in turn increase the likelihood that a mild or ambiguous provocation will be interpreted in a hostile fashion.
2. Aggressive (or hostile) emotion increases.
3. General arousal (e.g., heart rate) increases, which tends to increase the dominant behavioral tendency.
4. Youth learn new forms of aggressive behaviors by observing them, and will reenact them almost immediately afterwards if the situational context is sufficiently similar.

The Long-Term Impact of Media Violence

Repeated consumption of media violence over time increases aggression across a range to situations and across time because of several related factors.

1. It creates more positive attitudes, beliefs, and expectations regarding aggressive solutions to interpersonal problems. In other words, youth come to believe that aggression is normal, appropriate, and likely to succeed.

2. It also leads to the development of aggressive scripts, which are basically ways of thinking about how the social world works. Heavy media violence consumers tend to view the world in a more hostile fashion.

3. It decreases the cognitive accessibility of nonviolent ways to handle conflict. That is, it becomes harder to even think about nonviolent solutions.

4. It produces an emotional desensitization to aggression and violence. Normally, people have a pretty negative emotional reaction to conflict, aggression, and violence, and this can be seen in their physiological reactions to observation of violence (real or fictional, as in entertainment media). For example, viewing physical violence normally leads to increases in heart rate and blood pressure, as well as to certain brain wave patterns. Such normal negative emotional reactions tend to inhibit aggressive behavior, and can inspire helping behavior. Repeated consumption of media violence reduces these normal negative emotional reactions.

5. Repetition increases learning of any type of skill or way of thinking, to the point where that skill or way of thinking becomes fairly automatic. [This includes] learning how to aggress.

3. Is there a difference between the effects of TV/film violence versus video-game violence?

Most of the research has focused on TV/film violence (so-called "passive" media), mainly because they have been around so much longer than video games. However, the existing research literature on violent video games has yielded the same general types of effects as the TV and Cinema research. At a theoretical level, there are reasons to believe that violent video games may have a larger harmful effect than violent TV and film effects. This is a very difficult research question, and there currently is no definite answer. But, recent studies that directly compare passive screen media to video games tend to find bigger effects of violent video games.

Negative Effects of Violent Media

4. Is that why there have been so many school shootings by kids who play lots of violent video games? Can such games turn a normal, well-adjusted child or adolescent into a school shooter?

No, that would be an overstatement, one that mainstream media violence researchers do not make. The best way to think about this is the risk factor approach. There are three important points to keep in mind.

First, there are many causal risk factors involved in the development of a person who frequently behaves in an aggressive or violent manner. There are biological factors, family factors, neighborhood factors, and so on. Media violence is only one of the top dozen or so risk factors.

Second, extreme aggression, such as aggravated assault and homicide, typically occurs only when there are a number of risk factors present. In other words, none of the causal risk factors are "necessary and sufficient" causes of extreme aggression. Of course, cigarette smoking is not a necessary and sufficient cause of lung cancer, even though it is a major cause of it. People with only one risk factor seldom (I'm tempted to say "never") commit murder.

Third, consumption of media violence is the most common of all of the major risk factors for aggression in most modern societies. It also is the least expensive and easiest risk factor for parents to change. In sum, playing a lot of violent games is unlikely to turn a normal youth with zero or one or even two other risk factors into a killer. But regardless of how many other risk factors are present in a youth's life, playing a lot of violent games is likely to increase the frequency and the seriousness of his or her physical aggression, both in the short term and over time as the youth grows up.

5. Are some social groups more susceptible to the negative effects of violent video games than others? Are some groups immune to these effects?

There is some research suggesting that individuals who are already fairly aggressive may be more affected by consumption of violent video games, but it is not yet conclusive. Similarly, video game effects occasionally appear to be larger for males than females, but such findings are rare. Most studies find that males and females are equally affected, and that high and low aggressive individuals are equally affected. One additional point is worth remembering: Scientists have not been able to find any group of people who consistently appear immune to the negative effects of media violence or video game violence.

6. How important is the distinction between realistic violence versus fantasy violence?

This is an extremely important question because it is so frequently misunderstood. Many people, including psychiatrists and psychologists, tend to think: "Well, it is just a game, this boy (girl) is able to understand the difference between it and reality. Let us not worry about it." One of the great myths surrounding media violence is this notion that if the individual can distinguish between media violence and reality, then it can't have an adverse effect on that individual. Of course, the conclusion does not logically follow from the premise. And in fact, most of the studies that have demonstrated a causal link between exposure to media violence and subsequent aggressive behavior have been done with individuals who were fully aware that the observed media violence was not reality. For instance, many studies have used young adult participants who knew that the TV show, the movie clip, or the video game to which they were exposed was not "real." These studies still yielded the typical media violence effect on subsequent aggressive behavior.

7. Aren't there studies of violent video games that have found no significant effects on aggression?

Yes, such studies do exist. In any field of science, some studies will produce effects that differ from what most studies of that type find. If this weren't true, then one would need to perform only one study on a particular issue and we would have the "true" answer. Unfortunately, science is not that simple. . . .

Marketing Violence

8. But what about the claims made by the media industries and by some other media violence experts, who say that the existing research evidence shows no effects of violent media?

The various entertainment media industries have lots of money to spend on trying to convince the general public and political leaders that there is nothing to worry about. And they do spend large sums on this. Unlike the research community, which has no vested interest in the topic, the media industry is very concerned about profits and will do almost anything to protect those profits. A recent book by James Steyer titled *The Other Parent: The Inside Story of the Media's Effect on Our Children*, reveals much about how this works in the U.S. I suspect that most people would be shocked by many of the revelations contained in this book. I personally have witnessed media industry lobbyists lie about a factual issue, watched them get caught in that lie, and then seen the same lobbyist deliver the same lie to a different group a year later. So, one must distinguish between real vs. industry supported experts. . . .

9. Does violence sell?

Clearly, violence does sell, at least in the video game market. But it is not clear whether the dominance of violent video games is due to an inherent desire for such games, or whether this is merely the result of the fact that most marketing dollars are spent on promoting violent games instead of nonviolent ones. One great irony in all of this is the industry belief that violence is necessary in their product in order to make a profit. One result of that belief is that most of marketing efforts go into marketing violence. In fact, the media has seemingly convinced many people in the U.S. that they like only violent media products. But nonviolent and low violent products can be exciting, fun, and sell well. *Myst* is a good example of an early nonviolent video game that sold extremely well for quite some time. More recent examples include *The Sims*, many sports and racing games, and many simulation games. Interestingly, in some of our studies college students have to play nonviolent video games. Some of the these students report that they have never played nonviolent games, and are surprised to learn that they like some of the nonviolent ones as much as their violent games. . . .

10. So are video games basically bad for youth?

No, a better summary statement is that a well-designed video game is an excellent teaching tool. But what it teaches depends upon its content. Some games teach thinking skills. Some teach math. Some teach reading, or puzzle solving, or history. Some have been designed to teach kids how to manage specific illnesses, such as diabetes, asthma, and cancer. But all games teach something, and that "something" depends on what they require the player to practice. In short, there are many nonviolent games that are fun, exciting, and challenging. Children and adolescents (and adults) like them and can learn positive things from them. Some even get you to exercise muscles other than those in your hands. In moderation, such games are good for youth. But parents and educators need to check the content of the games they are considering for the youth in their care. You can't simply use the game ratings, because many games rated by the industry as appropriate for children and for teens contain lots of violence. But with a bit of parental effort, and some household rules about game-playing, the youth's gaming experience can be fun and positive.

| "*Whether or not violent video games cause harm to those who play them has been a subject of great debate for many years.*"

Violent Video Games Do Not Promote Teen Aggression and Violence

Serena Gordon

In the following viewpoint, Serena Gordon discusses biomedical research into whether or not violent video games cause aggression in teens. Although this has been the cause of many arguments, Gordon contends that it is unknown and inconclusive whether the video games promote violent behavior. She reports that a recent study shows that violent video games affect and change the brain function of teenagers, but it cannot yet be proven that such change causes the teens themselves to be violent. Serena Gordon is a HealthDay News *reporter.*

As you read, consider the following questions:

1. Who is Dr. Yang Wang?
2. What occurs with repeated violent video game play as stated in the article?

3. What can a parent do if they are concerned about their child's video game play, according to Tracy Dennis?

When young men who don't normally play a lot of video games are exposed to violent video games, changes occur in the way their brains function, new research shows.

Using functional magnetic resonance imaging (fMRI), scientists were able to document altered brain responses after video game play. What's more, some of those changes were still present a week later.

"We found that functioning has been changed in the brain by violent video games," said Dr. Yang Wang, an assistant research professor in the department of radiology and imaging sciences at Indiana University School of Medicine in Indianapolis. "We found that activation [of an area of the brain that controls emotion] is decreased after playing violent video games."

But, exactly what those changes mean, if anything, is still unknown.

Meanings of Brain Function Changes Are Unknown

"Clinically, we don't know what these changes mean, but it does affect your brain somehow," Wang said. "The pattern we found is similar to what we've seen in past research, and in adolescents is similar to what is seen in disruptive behavior disorders."

Tracy Dennis, a child development expert and an associate professor of psychology at Hunter College in New York City, said: "This study is a good first step. It shows that if you do something over and over again for a period of time, it will affect your brain. But, what that means in the real world isn't clear."

Wang is scheduled to present the findings Wednesday at the Radiological Society of North America's annual meeting this week in Chicago.

The Debate on Video Game Harm

Whether or not violent video games cause harm to those who play them has been a subject of great debate for many years. Although experts on both sides of the issue continue to disagree, there's little documented scientific evidence on what goes on in the brain during video game play.

In an attempt to provide some hard evidence, Wang and his colleagues recruited 22 healthy males between the ages of 18 and 29. These young men all reported low levels (less than one hour a week) of previous violent video game play.

The volunteers were randomly placed into one of two groups. One group was told to play a violent video game for about 10 hours at home in the first week, followed by a week of no violent video game play. The other group served as a control group and didn't play video games for the two-week study period.

All of the volunteers underwent three fMRIs: one at the start of the study, another a week later, and the final one two weeks later. During the fMRIs, the volunteers were given an emotional interference test and a cognitive inhibition counting task.

The men who played violent video games showed less activation in the left inferior frontal lobe during the emotional task, and less activation in the anterior cingulated cortex during the counting task, compared to their own baseline test and to the control group after one week.

Wang said those areas of the brain are important for controlling emotions and aggressive behavior.

More Research Is Needed

After the second week, when there was no video game play, the changes in the brain activation were reduced. Wang said the study wasn't designed to assess whether or not if someone continually plays violent video games, the changes to the brain become permanent at some point.

"That may be a question for future research," Wang noted.

"These changes don't necessarily mean the brain region isn't doing its job. There was decreased activity in the prefrontal cortex. Does that mean these men can't use that area as well, or could it mean it's become more efficient? You just don't know. You just know that they had a change in their brain," Dennis said.

If parents are concerned about their child's video game play, Dennis recommends using common sense. "Limit the amount they're playing. Don't sit a kid in front of violent video games for hours at a time," she advised.

Because this study was presented at a medical meeting, the data and conclusions should be viewed as preliminary until published in a peer-reviewed journal.

Periodical and Internet Sources Bibliography

The following articles have been chosen to supplement the diverse views presented in this chapter.

American Academy of Child and Adolescent Psychiatry	"Obesity in Children and Teens," *Facts for Families*, vol. 79, March 2011.
Rachel Grumman Bender	"Sneaky Signs of Teen Eating Disorders," March 8, 2011. www.everydayhealth.com.
Brad J. Bushman	"The Effects of Violent Video Games: Do They Affect Our Behavior?," 2012. www.ithp.org.
Alison Gopnik	"What's Wrong with the Teenage Mind?," *Wall Street Journal*, January 28, 2012.
Henry Jenkins	"Reality Bytes: Eight Myths About Violent Video Games Debunked," PBS. www.pbs.org.
Adam Liptak	"Justices Reject Ban on Violent Video Games for Children," *New York Times*, June 27, 2011. www.nytimes.com.
Jane McGonigal	"Video Games: An Hour a Day Is Key to Success in Life," *Huffington Post*, February 15, 2011. www.huffingtonpost.com.
Media Awareness Network	"Beauty and Body Image in the Media." www.media-awareness.ca.
Alice Park	"How Playing Violent Video Games May Change the Brain," December 2, 2011. www.healthland.time.com.
Kristen Stewart	"Teenage Depression: Are Girls at Greater Risk?," November 30, 2011. www.everydayhealth.com.
Shankar Vedantam	"It's a Duel: How Do Violent Video Games Affect Kids?," NPR, July 7, 2011. www.npr.org.

CHAPTER 2

How Does Substance Abuse Impact Teens?

Chapter Preface

According to a 2011 report by the National Center on Addiction and Substance Abuse, nearly half (46 percent) of all teens in the United States use and abuse substances that are illegal for them, particularly alcohol and marijuana. In 1973, President Richard Nixon declared the beginning of a War on Drugs. The War on Drugs had two main prongs: prohibition and education in the United States and interdiction and intervention abroad. Since that time, the rates of teen drug and alcohol use have fluctuated, sometimes up and sometimes down. According to the 2011 national Monitoring the Future survey, teen tobacco use in 2011 decreased significantly and use of hard drugs and alcohol declined slightly, while the rate of marijuana use by teens increased. National polls have shown a consistent increase in the percentage of people who think that marijuana should be legalized, from 44 percent in 2009, to 46 percent in 2010, and 50 percent in 2011, according to the Gallup poll. In March 2012, conservative Christian minister Pat Robertson added his name to this group. Seventy percent of respondents nationally approve of medical uses for marijuana. These changes in attitudes lead many to believe the War on Drugs is not working, at least as it pertains to marijuana.

According to the Office of Drug Control Policy, the federal government in 2010 spent more than $15 billion on the War on Drugs, and state and local governments spent at least $25 billion. A significant portion of this $40 billion goes to drug education programs in schools, but the question arises: Do these programs work? The largest national drug education program is Drug Abuse Resistance Education (DARE), which began in Los Angeles in 1983. It is currently taught in 80 percent of school districts nationwide, and it receives between 1 and 1.3 billion dollars a year from federal and local sources. DARE is a police-led series of classroom lessons taught anytime between kindergarten to twelfth grade, though in many areas it is focused on fifth grade classes. DARE promotes the philosophy of abstinence, believing that kids will refuse to try drugs if they can be educated about how bad drugs are for them. Though there is no social science evidence that DARE has made a positive difference in deterring drug use, it continues to be embraced by law enforcement and funded by politicians as a healthy part of adolescent education.

The criticism of DARE has been particularly harsh in recent years. Scholars and educators attack DARE, while law enforcement and elected politicians defend it. As scholar David J. Hansen notes, "Scientific evaluation studies have consistently shown that DARE is ineffective in reducing the use of alcohol and drugs and is sometimes even counterproductive—worse than doing nothing. That's the conclusion of the US General Accounting Office, the US Surgeon General, the National Academy of Sciences, and the US Department of Education, among many others." In spite of the criticism, DARE continues to thrive, largely because it is well liked by students, parents, and law enforcement officers who believe in the program's premises.

While DARE promotes abstention from drug use though education, the law enforcement approach kicks in when abstinence fails. Teens who are arrested for violating drug laws—and more than one hundred thousand teens were last year—frequently find themselves expelled or suspended from school and sent into drug treatment programs instead of jail. According to Charles Puzzanchera of the National Center for Juvenile Justice, the juvenile arrest rate for drug abuse violations is up 78 percent since 1990. These two approaches to teen substance abuse—abstinence through drug education and deterrence through legal punishment—are important contexts for understanding the issues in the following chapter.

"Teen users are at significantly higher risk of developing an addictive disorder compared to adults, and the earlier they began using, the higher their risk."

Teen Substance Use Often Leads to Addiction

National Center on Addiction and Substance Abuse

In the following viewpoint, the National Center on Addiction and Substance Abuse (CASA) contends that teen substance abuse and addiction have reached epidemic proportions, with very high rates of teenagers meeting the criteria for having a substance use disorder. In spite of the high costs to society, CASA finds that both media glamorization and parental indifference contribute to the problem. CASA, based out of Columbia University in New York City, has been devoted to publicizing and combating the problems of addiction in US society for the past twenty years.

As you read, consider the following questions:

1. According to the viewpoint, what percentage of high school students who are current users have a clinically-defined addiction to cigarettes, alcohol, or drugs?

2. Name one of the three substances noted in the viewpoint that have increased in use in recent years.

3. What percentage of parents believe that marijuana is a harmless drug, according to a study cited in the viewpoint?

This report finds that adolescent smoking, drinking, misusing prescription drugs and using illegal drugs is, by any measure, a public health problem of epidemic proportion, presenting clear and present danger to millions of America's teenagers and severe and expensive long-range consequences for our entire population. This report is a wake-up call for all of us, regardless of whether we seek to win the future by investing in our youth or seek to cut public spending to avoid a back-breaking financial burden on our children and grandchildren. The findings and recommendations in this report offer common ground and opportunity to help achieve both objectives.

This report finds that:

- Three-fourths of high school students (75.6 percent, 10.0 million) have used addictive substances including cigarettes, alcohol, marijuana or cocaine.
- Almost half of high school students (46.1 percent, 6.1 million) are current users of these substances.
- Of high school students who have ever smoked a cigarette, had a drink of alcohol or used other drugs, 19.4 percent have a clinical substance use disorder, [that is, they meet clinical criteria for dependence, also referred to as addiction in this report] as do 33.3 percent of current users.

And these estimates are low; none include adolescents who are incarcerated in the juvenile justice system or the large numbers of adolescents who have dropped out of high school. Rates of substance use and substance use disorders are even higher in these populations than among high school students generally.

The Link Between Use and Addiction

Teen users are at significantly higher risk of developing an addictive disorder compared to adults, and the earlier they began using, the higher their risk. Nine out of 10 people who meet the clinical criteria for substance use disorders involving nicotine, alcohol or other drugs began smoking, drinking or using other drugs before they turned 18. People who begin using any addictive substance before age 15 are six and a half times as likely to develop a substance use disorder as those who delay use until age 21 or older (28.1 percent vs. 4.3 percent).

Alcohol is the most preferred addictive substance among high school students:

- 72.5 percent of high school students have drunk alcohol,
- 46.3 percent have smoked cigarettes,
- 36.8 percent have used marijuana and
- 14.8 percent have misused controlled prescription drugs.

Two-thirds (65.1 percent) of high school students have used more than one substance.

The fact that 75.6 percent of high school students have used addictive substances and 46.1 percent are current users dwarfs the prevalence rates of many other risky health behaviors considered to be of epidemic proportion among teens in the U.S. For example, 34.2 percent of teens are overweight or obese; 18.3 percent have ever experienced symptoms of depression; and 28.1 percent of 9th graders and 19.9 percent of 12th graders have been victims of bullying. Substance use also frequently co-occurs with these and other health problems that teens face.

Consequences of Teen Substance Use

The immediate consequences of teen substance use are devastating, ranging from injuries and unintended pregnancies; to medical conditions such as asthma, depression, anxiety, psychosis and impaired brain function; to reduced academic performance and educational achievement; to criminal involvement and even death.

And, these consequences extend beyond teen users to those who breathe in their cigarette smoke; those assaulted, injured or killed by teens who are drunk or high; those who contract sexually transmitted diseases or experience unplanned pregnancies; and to babies born to teen mothers who smoke, drink or use other drugs during pregnancy.

It does not take heavy or dependent use to experience life-altering and potentially fatal consequences. Driving a car under the influence of alcohol or other drugs can lead to disability or death. One occasion of drinking or other drug use can result in a dangerous fight or having unprotected sex. It can take as few as one or two episodes of smoking to show symptoms of nicotine dependence or one dose of cocaine to die from a heart attack. And all of these tragic outcomes also create substantial costs to society.

Financial Costs of Teen Substance Use

The financial costs of teen substance use and addiction include, for example, an estimated $68.0 billion associated with underage drinking alone and $14.4 billion associated with substance-related juvenile justice programs annually. In the long run, the consequences of adolescent substance use and addiction place enormous burdens on our health care, criminal justice, family court, education and social service systems.

Total costs to federal, state and local governments of substance use among the entire U.S. population are at least $467.7 billion per year—almost $1,500 for every person in America—driven primarily by those who began their use as teens. These costs are the result of accidents, diseases, crimes, child neglect and abuse, unplanned pregnancies, homelessness, unemployment and other outcomes of our failure to prevent substance use and treat this health condition. Addiction, whether to nicotine, alcohol or other drugs, is a complex brain disease that can be treated, but when left untreated, the consequences and their costs escalate.

The Making of an Epidemic

This report finds that the tragedy is not that we don't know what to do; rather, it is that we simply fail to do it. We know that risky substance use and addiction are the leading causes of preventable death and disability in the United States, and in most cases it begins in the teen years. Adolescence is, in fact, *the* critical period for the onset of substance use and its potentially debilitating consequences for two reasons:

- The regions of the brain that are critical to decision making, judgment, impulse control, emotion and memory are not yet fully developed in adolescence, making teens more prone than adults to taking risks, including experimenting with tobacco, alcohol and other drugs.
- Because the teen brain is still developing, addictive substances physically alter its structure and function faster and more intensely than in adults, interfering with brain development, further impairing judgment and heightening the risk of addiction.

While adolescence itself increases the chances that teens will use addictive substances, American culture further increases that risk. Teens are highly vulnerable to the wide-ranging social influences that subtly condone or more overtly encourage their use of these substances. These influences include the acceptance of substance use by parents, schools and communities; pervasive advertising of these products; media portrayals of substance use as benign, or even glamorous, fun and relaxing; and the widespread availability of tobacco, alcohol, marijuana and controlled prescription drugs. Our teens are awash in a sea of addictive substances, while adults send mixed messages at best, wink and look the other way, or blatantly condone or promote their use. In so doing, we normalize behavior that undermines the health and futures of our teens.

Adding to the recipe for teen substance use, many teens have other challenges in their lives that make them more in-

A Dirty Delivery System

Suppose you are watching television and you suddenly see a message: "Traces of *cyanide, mercury, acetone,* and *ammonia* have been discovered in a widely consumed commercial product." When this message was shown on French television, about a million viewers called the toll-free number given on the screen to get more information. Those who were able to complete the call discovered the answer: cigarettes.

Smokers smoke for the effect of nicotine, but they get a lot more. Manufacturers add chemicals to make cigarettes taste and smell better. Some of these—such as chocolate, caffeine, and yeast—are safe as foods, but they change when heated and burned. Cigarettes are a dirty delivery system, with more than 4,000 compounds present in the smoke that is inhaled to produce a pleasurable feeling.

As mentioned earlier, many chemicals are added to tobacco when cigarettes are made. One of these, ammonia, is added to cigarette tobacco to release more nicotine. Among the toxic chemicals that form when a cigarette burns are tar particles that make up the visible part of the smoke. The lungs of a person who smokes a pack or more of cigarettes a day is exposed to a total of one and one-half pounds of gooey black tar a year.

Margaret O. Hyde and John F. Setaro, MD, Smoking 101: An Overview for Teens. *Minneapolis: Twenty-First Century Books, 2006 p. 23.*

clined to use addictive substances, more vulnerable to the ubiquitous cultural influences promoting use or that hike the risk of progression from substance use to addiction. These challenges include being the victim of neglect, abuse or other trauma, suffering from mental health disorders that frequently co-occur with substance use and inheriting a genetic predisposition to addiction.

The science of addiction and evidence of its consequences is clear enough to conclude that there is no recommended level of safe use of addictive substances by teens. . . .

Progress Has Stalled

Despite considerable declines in overall reported rates of current substance use since 1999, progress appears to have stalled and rates may once again be on the rise. The use of smokeless tobacco has been increasing since 2003. Declines in past 30 day cigarette smoking are slowing significantly, and national data suggest that current use of marijuana and controlled prescription drugs may be inching up.

The overall decline in substance use rates also may obfuscate dangerous patterns of substance use; for example, high school students drink more drinks when they drink (4.9 drinks per day) than any other age group, including 18–25 year olds (4.4 drinks per day).

While most teens responding to CASA's survey of high school students conducted for this study report that they believe substance use to be very dangerous, almost half of them are current users. Further, a quarter of them (24.7 percent) see marijuana as a harmless drug and 16.9 percent think of it as a medicine. Teens who hold favorable views of the benefits of substance use—such as being cool or popular, weight control, self-medication, stress relief or coping—are more likely to smoke, drink and use other drugs than those who hold less favorable beliefs or stronger perceptions of risk.

The High Risk of Addiction

One in eight high school students (11.9 percent, 1.6 million) have a diagnosable clinical substance use disorder involving nicotine, alcohol or other drugs. Because the adolescent brain is more sensitive to the addictive properties of nicotine, alcohol and other drugs, the younger a person is when he or she begins to use addictive substances, the greater the risk of developing the disease of addiction.

Every year that the onset of substance use is delayed until the mid-20s—about the time when the human brain is more fully developed—the risk of developing a substance use disorder is reduced. One in four people who used *any* addictive substance before they turned 18 have a substance use disorder, compared with one in 25 who first used any of these substances at age 21 or older.

Substance Use Affects Safety, Health, and Academic Performance

Teen substance use contributes to some of the most glaring barriers to health and productivity facing the current generation of teenagers in the United States. For example:

- Teen tobacco, alcohol and marijuana users are at least twice as likely as nonusers to have poor grades and teen marijuana users are approximately twice as likely as nonusers to drop out of high school.
- In 2009, one in 10 (9.7 percent) high school students reported driving after drinking alcohol in the past month.
- More than one in five (21.6 percent) sexually-active high school students report having used alcohol or other drugs before their last sexual experience; one in five teens and young adults report having unprotected sex after drinking or using other drugs.
- In 2009, 32.0 percent of all substance-related reports in emergency department visits made by patients ages 12 to 17 were alcohol related and 18.7 percent were marijuana related.
- Substance use is a major contributor to the three leading causes of death among adolescents—accidents, homicides

and suicides—and increases the risk of numerous potentially fatal health conditions, including cancers, heart disease and respiratory illnesses.

- Smoking is related to impaired lung growth, asthma-related symptoms and declines in lung function in adolescence; regular cigarette smoking increases the risk of lung cancer, breast cancer, emphysema, bronchial disorders and cardiovascular diseases.

- Alcohol-induced damage has been observed in the brains of binge-drinking teens. Teens with alcohol use disorders have more self-reported health problems (including problems with sleep, eating and vision) and more abnormalities during physical examinations (including in the abdominal region as well as in their respiratory and cardiovascular systems) than those without alcohol use disorders.

- Heavy or chronic marijuana use is associated with a host of cognitive impairments and with structural and functional brain changes. Regular use of marijuana can hike the risk of respiratory illnesses including chronic cough, bronchitis and lung infections.

Even relatively low levels of substance use can have disastrous consequences for teens, including accidents, violence, unsafe sexual activity, cardiac and respiratory problems and even death.

The consequences of adolescent substance use extend to all teens, even those who are not using. A significant proportion of high school students reports knowing someone personally who has gotten into trouble with parents, their school or the authorities (41.0 percent); who has gotten into an accident (26.8 percent); whose ability to perform school or work activities has been disturbed (24.5 percent); who has been injured or harassed (19.4 percent each); who has had an unintended pregnancy (13.8 percent); who has experienced physical abuse (11.1 percent); and who has been sexually assaulted or raped (7.0 percent) due to someone else's substance use.

US Culture Drives Teen Substance Use

Strong parental disapproval of substance use can help offset cultural messages promoting substance use, but too many parents by their own attitudes or behaviors further increase the chances that their teens will use:

- Nearly half (46.1 percent) of children under age 18 (34.4 million) live in a household where someone age 18 or older engages in risky substance use; 45.4 percent (33.9 million) live with a *parent* who is a risky substance user.
- More than one in six (17.8 percent) children under age 18 (13.3 million) live in a household where someone age 18 or older has a substance use disorder; 16.9 percent (12.6 million) live with a *parent* who has the disorder.
- Less than half (42.6 percent) of parents list refraining from smoking cigarettes, drinking alcohol, using marijuana, misusing prescription drugs or using other illicit drugs as one of their top three concerns for their teens, and 20.8 percent characterize marijuana as a harmless drug. . . .

The Media Affect Teen Substance Use

Depictions of smoking and drinking in television shows and movies popular with teens also are pervasive. The odds of becoming a tobacco user are more than doubled by exposure to tobacco marketing and media images of tobacco use. Alcohol advertising is related to young people's attitudes and expectations regarding drinking and to their risk of alcohol use.

If teens exposed to these messages decide to try smoking, drinking or using other drugs, they have little trouble obtaining these products. The majority of 10th graders say that it would be easy for them to get cigarettes (76.1 percent), alcohol (80.9 percent) or marijuana (69.3 percent). The most common sources of tobacco, alcohol and other drugs are friends and family.

| *"Compared to other substances, marijuana is not very addicting."*

Teen Substance Use Seldom Leads to Addiction

Jann Gumbiner

In the following viewpoint, Jann Gumbiner discusses whether recreational use of marijuana causes addiction or dependency. Gumbiner claims that the majority of people who use marijuana try it experimentally and never become addicted. Although it is said that today's pot is stronger, Gumbiner cites research that suggests marijuana is not addictive for the majority of users and using it does not necessarily lead to dependence. Jann Gumbiner is a licensed psychologist and clinical professor at the University of California, Irvine's College of Medicine.

As you read, consider the following questions:

1. What are some withdrawal symptoms listed by the author?
2. Is it harder to quit cigarettes or to quit smoking pot, according to the article?
3. What percentage of recreational users does Gumbiner state will "develop problems severe enough to impair their work and relationships"?

A realistic concern for recreational users of marijuana is whether or not they will become addicted. There are no easy answers to this question. In my opinion, the most unbiased book on this and other related topics is *The Science of Marijuana* (2008) . . . by Leslie L. Iverson, a professor of pharmacology at the University of Cambridge in England. In the book, he reviews decades of international research on marijuana, both laboratory research and survey research. Based on his review of the scientific literature, between 10 to 30 percent of regular users will develop dependency. Only about 9 percent will have a serious addiction. . . .

The large majority of people who try marijuana do it experimentally and never become addicted. Unlike other substances, pot has very few severe withdrawal symptoms and most people can quit rather easily. When present, withdrawal symptoms might include: anxiety, depression, nausea, sleep disturbances and GI [gastrointestinal] problems.

Marijuana Is Not Very Addicting

Compared to other substances, marijuana is not very addicting. It is estimated that 32 percent of tobacco users will become addicted, 23 percent of heroin users, 17 percent of cocaine users, and 15 percent of alcohol users. Cocaine and heroin are more physically harmful, and nicotine is much more addictive. It is much harder to quit smoking cigarettes than it is to quit smoking pot.

Recreational users of the past are often compared to todays smokers. The smokers, the times and the pot are all different. According to Iversen, marijuana was introduced in the US during the 1960s by Vietnam [War] vets. This was a time of social upheaval and strong anti-war sentiment. Youth were rebellious and experimental pot smokers. Today's youth are different. They are mainstream. Interestingly, many of today's young smokers are children of the previous generation of smokers. And, my generation of marijuana smokers quit relatively easily when they became parents and homeowners.

It is often said that today's pot is stronger. I am not sure how anybody could know this. Readers, if you know please tell me. Are there studies comparing THC [tetrahydrocannabinol, the active compound in marijuana] content of 1970 pot with 2010 pot? How could this even be possible on a large scale? Does somebody still have some 1970 pot sitting around or are we relying on old memories? The only thing that I can surmise is that the marijuana that is carefully cultivated indoors these days is more potent than previous strains. In fact, this brings to mind one of my greatest frustrations. In California, small amounts of marijuana are legal for people with 215 cards [medical marijuana ID cards] but it is not regulated. So, how does anybody know how much THC they are smoking? Do they even know where it was grown and how much pesticide it contains? For example, when I buy Advil in the supermarket, I know that I am getting 200 mg capsules.

Experienced Users Regulate Their THC Intake

In spite of different strains of marijuana containing different amounts of THC, experienced smokers are able to control their high. An interesting study reported in Iversen's book claims that regular users know how to inhale in a way that regulates THC content. A study was conducted where experienced smokers were given joints with either 1 percent or 4 percent levels of THC. The subjects were blind to experimental conditions so they didn't know the THC content of the joint. Without knowing which joint they were smoking, the smokers automatically adjusted their inhaling to reach about the same degree of high and THC absorption. They did this by taking longer and harder draws on the weaker joint and breathing in more air with the more potent joint.

So, to wrap up, is marijuana addictive? For most people, no. About 10 percent of recreational users will develop problems serve enough to impair their work and relationships. Many more will come to depend on pot for relaxation and social purposes. This will be problematic if they don't learn more effective coping mechanisms and come to rely on marijuana instead of solving their problems. When ready, most people will be able to quit with only mild withdrawal symptoms. And, compared to other recreational drugs, marijuana is relatively harmless. But, it is not completely harmless. And . . . what is more serious than its addictive consequences are the legal ones. This relatively harmless herbal plant is unregulated and illegal in the US.

> *"Evidence suggests that, compared with their nonsmoking peers, students who smoke marijuana tend to get lower grades and are more likely to drop out of high school."*

Marijuana Use Is Harmful

National Institute on Drug Abuse

In the following viewpoint, marijuana is examined from a health and social perspective. Marijuana is found to be harmful to memory, coordination, and respiratory functions, and it is found to raise the risk of psychotic reactions, heart attacks, cancer, and addiction, the viewpoint states. For teens, the use of marijuana is associated with a number of poor outcomes, including reductions in educational attainment and income, according to the viewpoint. Sponsored by the National Institutes of Health, the National Institute on Drug Abuse (NIDA) is a federal agency dedicated to fighting drug abuse and addiction through education.

As you read, consider the following questions:

1. Name one task that requires concentration and can be disrupted by use of marijuana, as noted in the viewpoint.
2. According to the viewpoint, animal studies have shown

"Research Reports: Marijuana Abuse," National Institute on Drug Abuse, September 2010. www.drugabuse.gov. Courtesy of the National Institute on Drug Abuse.

that marijuana causes memory impairment as it affects what part of the brain?

3. The viewpoint contends that withdrawal from marijuana addiction has symptoms similar to withdrawal from addiction to what other drug?

As THC [tetrahydrocannabinol, the active compound in marijuana] enters the brain, it causes the user to feel euphoric—or high—by acting on the brain's reward system, which is made up of regions that govern the response to pleasurable things like sex and chocolate, as well as to most drugs of abuse. THC activates the reward system in the same way that nearly all drugs of abuse do: by stimulating brain cells to release the chemical dopamine.

The Effects of Marijuana on the Brain

Along with euphoria, relaxation is another frequently reported effect in human studies. Other effects, which vary dramatically among different users, include heightened sensory perception (e.g., brighter colors), laughter, altered perception of time, and increased appetite. After a while, the euphoria subsides, and the user may feel sleepy or depressed. Occasionally, marijuana use may produce anxiety, fear, distrust, or panic.

Marijuana use impairs a person's ability to form new memories and to shift focus. THC also disrupts coordination and balance by binding to receptors in the cerebellum and basal ganglia—parts of the brain that regulate balance, posture, coordination, and reaction time. Therefore, learning, doing complicated tasks, participating in athletics, and driving are also affected.

Marijuana users who have taken large doses of the drug may experience an acute psychosis, which includes hallucinations, delusions, and a loss of the sense of personal identity. Although the specific causes of these symptoms remain unknown, they appear to occur more frequently when a high dose of cannabis is consumed in food or drink rather than smoked. Such short-term psychotic reactions to high concentrations of THC are distinct from longer-lasting, schizophrenia-like disorders that have been associated with the use of cannabis in vulnerable individuals.

Our understanding of marijuana's long-term brain effects is limited. Research findings on how chronic cannabis use affects brain *structure*, for example, have been inconsistent. It may be that the effects are too subtle for reliable detection by current techniques. A similar challenge arises in studies of the effects of chronic marijuana use on brain *function*. Although imaging studies (functional MRI; fMRI) in chronic users do show some consistent alterations, the relation of these changes to cognitive functioning is less clear. This uncertainty may stem from confounding factors such as other drug use, residual drug effects (which can occur for at least 24 hours in chronic users), or withdrawal symptoms in long-term chronic users.

How Marijuana Impairs Memory

Memory impairment from marijuana use occurs because THC alters how information is processed in the hippocampus, a brain area responsible for memory formation.

Most of the evidence supporting this assertion comes from animal studies. For example, rats exposed to THC in utero, soon after birth, or during adolescence, show notable problems with specific learning/memory tasks later in life. Moreover, cognitive impairment in adult rats is associated with structural and functional changes in the hippocampus from THC exposure during adolescence.

As people age, they lose neurons in the hippocampus, which decreases their ability to learn new information. Chronic THC exposure may hasten age-related loss of hippocampal neurons. In one study, rats exposed to THC every day for 8 months (approximately 30 percent of their life-span) showed a level of nerve cell loss (at 11 to 12 months of age) that equaled that of unexposed animals twice their age.

Teen Marijuana Use Has Risks

Research paints a grim picture for marijuana users who start at a young age:

- Teens using marijuana before age 18 are two to four times more likely to develop psychosis as young adults compared to those who do not.
- The teen brain is much more vulnerable to addiction. One in 6 kids who try marijuana before age 18 will either abuse it or become addicted to it compared with 1 in 25 adults.
- Studies show that heavy doses of THC, the key chemical in marijuana, during adolescence change the way the brain develops. In particular, marijuana's harmful effects strike the hippocampus, which is critical for learning and memory.

Katie Kerwin McCrimmon, "Research Shows Adverse Effects of Marijuana on Teens as Drug Use Among Student Appears to Be Rising," February 22, 2012. www.ednewscolorado.org.

An enduring question in the field is whether individuals who quit marijuana, even after long-term, heavy use, can recover some of their cognitive abilities. One study reports that the ability of long-term heavy marijuana users to recall words from a list was still impaired 1 week after they quit using, but returned to normal by 4 weeks. However, another study found that marijuana's effects on the brain can build up and deteriorate critical life skills over time. Such effects may be worse in those with other mental disorders, or simply by virtue of the normal aging process.

Marijuana's Effects on General Physical Health

Within a few minutes after inhaling marijuana smoke, an individual's heart rate speeds up, the bronchial passages relax and become enlarged, and blood vessels in the eyes expand, making the eyes look red. The heart rate—normally 70 to 80 beats per minute—may increase by 20 to 50 beats per minute, or may even double in some cases. Taking other drugs with marijuana can amplify this effect.

Limited evidence suggests that a person's risk of heart attack during the first hour after smoking marijuana is four times his or her usual risk. This observation could be partly explained by marijuana raising blood pressure (in some cases) and heart rate and reducing the blood's capacity to carry oxygen. Such possibilities need to be examined more closely, particularly since current marijuana users include adults from the baby boomer generation, who may have other cardiovascular risks that may increase their vulnerability.

Consequences of Marijuana Abuse

Acute (present during intoxication)
- Impairs short-term memory
- Impairs attention, judgment, and other cognitive functions
- Impairs coordination and balance
- Increases heart rate
- Psychotic episodes

Persistent (lasting longer than intoxication, but may not be permanent)
- Impairs memory and learning skills

• Sleep impairment

Long-term (cumulative effects of chronic abuse)
• Can lead to addiction
• Increases risk of chronic cough, bronchitis
• Increases risk of schizophrenia in vulnerable individuals
• May increase risk of anxiety, depression, and amotivational syndrome

Marijuana Causes Potential Respiratory Problems

The smoke of marijuana, like that of tobacco, consists of a toxic mixture of gases and particulates, many of which are known to be harmful to the lungs. Someone who smokes marijuana regularly may have many of the same respiratory problems that tobacco smokers do, such as daily cough and phlegm production, more frequent acute chest illnesses, and a greater risk of lung infections. Even infrequent marijuana use can cause burning and stinging of the mouth and throat, often accompanied by a heavy cough. One study found that extra sick days used by frequent marijuana smokers were often because of respiratory illnesses.

In addition, marijuana has the *potential* to promote cancer of the lungs and other parts of the respiratory tract because it contains irritants and carcinogens—up to 70 percent more than tobacco smoke. It also induces high levels of an enzyme that converts certain hydrocarbons into their cancer-causing form, which could accelerate the changes that ultimately produce malignant cells. And since marijuana smokers generally inhale more deeply and hold their breath longer than tobacco smokers, the lungs are exposed longer to carcinogenic smoke. However, while several lines of evidence have suggested that marijuana use may lead to lung cancer, the supporting evidence isnconclusive. The presence of an unidentified active ingredient in cannabis smoke having protective properties—if corroborated and properly characterized—could help explain the inconsistencies and modest findings. . . .

Is Marijuana Addictive?

Long-term marijuana use can lead to addiction; that is, people have difficulty controlling their drug use and cannot stop even though it interferes with many aspects of their lives. It is estimated that 9 percent of people who use marijuana will become dependent on it. The number goes up to about 1 in 6 in those who start using young (in their teens) and to 25–50 percent among daily users. Moreover, a study of over 300 fraternal and identical twin pairs found that the twin who had used marijuana before the age of 17 had elevated rates of other drug use and drug problems later on, compared with their twin who did not use before age 17.

According to the 2008 NSDUH [National Survey on Drug Use and Health], marijuana accounted for 4.2 million of the estimated 7 million Americans dependent on or abusing illicit drugs. In 2008, approximately 15 percent of people entering drug abuse treatment programs reported marijuana as their primary drug of abuse; 61 percent of persons under 15 reported marijuana as their primary drug of abuse, as did 56 percent of those 15 to 19 years old.

Marijuana addiction is also linked to a withdrawal syndrome similar to that of nicotine withdrawal, which can make it hard to quit. People trying to quit report irritability, sleeping difficulties, craving, and anxiety. They also show increased aggression on psychological tests, peaking approximately 1 week after they last used the drug.

Marijuana Affects School, Work, and Social Life

Research has shown that marijuana's negative effects on attention, memory, and learning can last for days or weeks after the acute effects of the drug wear off. Consequently, someone who smokes marijuana daily may be functioning at a reduced intellectual level most or all of the time. Not surprisingly, evidence suggests that, compared with their nonsmoking peers, students who smoke marijuana tend to get lower grades and are more likely to drop out of high school. A meta-analysis of 48 relevant studies—one of the most thorough performed to date—found cannabis use to be associated consistently with reduced educational attainment (e.g., grades and chances of graduating). However, a *causal* relationship is not yet proven between cannabis use by young people and psychosocial harm.

That said, marijuana users themselves report poor outcomes on a variety of life satisfaction and achievement measures. One study compared current and former long-term heavy users of marijuana with a control group who reported smoking cannabis at least once in their lives but not more than 50 times. Despite similar education and income backgrounds, significant differences were found in educational attainment: fewer of the heavy users of cannabis completed college, and more had yearly household incomes of less than $30,000. When asked how marijuana affected their cognitive abilities, career achievements, social lives, and physical and mental health, the majority of heavy cannabis users reported the drug's negative effects on all of these measures. In addition, several studies have linked workers' marijuana smoking with increased absences, tardiness, accidents, workers' compensation claims, and job turnover. For example, a study among postal workers found that employees who tested positive for marijuana on a pre-employment urine drug test had 55 percent more industrial accidents, 85 percent more injuries, and a 75-percent increase in absenteeism compared with those who tested negative for marijuana use.

"Teens are using cigarettes and alcohol less, but they are smoking more marijuana . . . because they do not perceive it to be as harmful as did teens in the past."

Teens Are Choosing Marijuana over More Harmful Substances

Kristen Gwynne

In the following viewpoint, Kristen Gwynne argues that the results of the "2011 Monitoring the Future Survey" on teen drug use show more teens are exhibiting good judgment about their substance use choices. Because teen rates of cigarette and alcohol use have gone down, while the rate of marijuana use has gone up, Gwynne contends that teens are becoming more educated about the associated risks of various substances. In her view, teen drug education should focus on harm reduction rather than complete abstinence. Gwynne is a reporter and assistant editor at Alternet.org.

As you read, consider the following questions:

1. Of the three most commonly used substances—alcohol, cigarettes, and marijuana—which one is the least harmful to health and least addictive, according to the viewpoint?

2. According to the viewpoint, what recent development concerning marijuana has promoted the perception that marijuana is not very harmful?

3. The viewpoint suggests that the emphasis on marijuana use should be replaced by an emphasis on which more harmful form of drug abuse?

The National Institute of Drug Abuse (NIDA) released the results of its 2011 Monitoring the Future Survey of teen drug use, and guess what: Teens are using cigarettes and alcohol less, but they are smoking more marijuana. What's more, they're smoking more weed because they do not perceive it to be as harmful as did teens in the past. Teens' level of "associated risk" with marijuana use has gone down over time, and marijuana is, indeed, less harmful than alcohol and cigarettes: This could be an argument for more honest drug education in schools.

The Associated Risk of Drug Use

Associated risk is the danger or harm believed to be a consequence of drug use. If associated risk for a particular substance goes up, more people are reporting that they consider using that drug to be a threat. In other words, as associated risk goes down, more people are saying the drug in question is not that bad. According to the NIDA study, a decline in marijuana's associated risk contributed to teens smoking more pot, while drinking less alcohol and smoking fewer cigarettes. Thus, many teens actually showed good judgement, by using available information to determine the danger posed by particular substances, and making smart decisions accordingly.

According to the study, about 25% of teens surveyed said they tried marijuana at least once last year, a statistically significant rise of about 4% since 2007. Additionally, 6.6% of 12th graders also admitted to smoking weed daily.

Frequent marijuana use is the highest it has been since 1981, but cigarette and alcohol use also reached historic lows. 11.7 percent of U.S. teens reported having smoked a cigarette in the last 30 days, compared to 12.8 percent in 2010. According to the report, a twenty-year gradual decline in alcohol use continued into 2011, and the decrease in that year alone was also significant:

> Over the past 20 years, from 1991 to 2011, the proportion of 8th graders reporting any use of alcohol in the prior 30 days has fallen by about half (from 25% to 13%), among 10th graders by more than one third (from 43% to 27%), and among 12th graders by about one fourth (from 54% to 40%).

Perceptions of the Harm and Benefit of Drugs

These findings are important, as alcohol and cigarettes are more deadly and addictive than pot. The report acknowledged that decreases in associated risk may play a factor in the increases in marijuana use. The decline in teens' perception of marijuana's harmfulness could be linked to public discussion of medical marijuana dispensaries and the ongoing debate about the medical benefits of marijuana. Thus, the study's own data proves what NIDA and other drug war institutions incessantly deny: Knowledge—even if it shows the benefits of a drug—matters. Give young people accurate information, and they will use it to make better decisions that result in less harm to themselves, because teens, like everybody else, do not actually want to get hurt or become addicts.

This is the importance of harm reduction education. Understanding the varying addictive nature and likelihood of overdose or impurity of different drugs will help teens to make smarter decisions when they begin to experiment. Giving students honest information about drugs, like appropriate dosage, and providing information about safe injection (or other methods of use), does not necessarily ensure that they will use drugs.

It does, however, increase the odds that they will use drugs safely, and reduce the likelihood of experiencing the harms associated with drugs. But to win the trust of young people so that they take this information seriously, educators must also be honest about the harm or risk associated with different drugs, and it's not one size fits all.

Increased Marijuana Use Is Beneficial

Though marijuana is a much safer drug than cigarettes or alcohol, not many officials are recognizing that marijuana's increase in use may have been a good thing, as it appears to be contributing to historic lows in cigarette and alcohol use. According to the *New York Times*, R. Gil Kerlikowske, the federal drug czar, said he believed increasing prevalence of medical marijuana contributed to a rise in teens' marijuana use—but not in a positive way.

"These last couple years, the amount of attention that's been given to medical marijuana has been huge," he told the *New York Times*. "And when I've done focus groups with high school students in states where medical marijuana is legal, they say, 'Well, if it's called medicine and it's given to patients by caregivers, then that's really the wrong message for us as high school students.'"

The context of the article suggests that Kerlikowske is implying that medical marijuana, though only available to card carrying adults at least 18 or 21 years old, has not only made pot easier to get, but has also made weed seem safer than he would like students to believe. To the disadvantage of his argument, pot has never killed anyone, and medical marijuana shows benefits for people living with glaucoma, AIDS, cancer, multiple sclerosis, and PTSD. And while pot may be more available in states where it is legal for medical reasons, in recent years, pot's associated risk has decreased more substantially than its availability has risen.

Additionally, recent data released by the Institute for the Study of Labor in Bonn, Germany—a research center for science, politics, and business—showed no evidence that the availability of medical marijuana influenced teens' use. What the study did find is that marijuana use is higher among adults in states where voters supported the legislation, and that the increase in use is actually beneficial: Researchers conducted that smoking more and drinking less contributed to a 9% decrease in traffic fatalities.

Teens Need Education Not Prohibition

And still, rather than accept the reality that teens always have, and always will, experiment with drugs, NIDA is calling its new marijuana statistics "depressing." NIDA and Kerlikowske are, in effect, advocating for prohibition and the limitation of information to explain only the most negative effects of drugs, even though some are more dangerous, or better for you, than others, rather than providing education that helps teens understand their health options, and ways of reducing the harm of drugs.

Last year [2010], 11.4% of 12th grade students smoked synthetic marijuana like K2 and Spice, sold previously in head shops and gas stations, until many states banned them. . . . [In December 2011], the House of Representatives voted to ban more than 40 substances found in once legal synthetic drugs. Their focus was on fake pot and bath salts, which are not a tub accessory, but research chemicals that mimic the highs of cocaine or meth amphetamine. . . .

Controlling Synthetic Marijuana

In a press release, Lloyd Johnston, the principal investigator of the study, said about synthetic marijuana, "Next year's results should tell us a lot more about how successful these new control efforts are. . . . We know that the great majority of those who have used synthetic marijuana also used regular marijuana during the year, as well as a number of other drugs."

"We know that any substance that is legally available is more widely used," Kerlikowske told the *Los Angeles Times*.

Even if that were true by all accounts, and more people were smoking fake pot than the real stuff (which, as even this study showed, they're not), this argument would be a great reason to

"Go over there and say something . . . ," cartoon by Terry Wise. www.CartoonStock.com.

legalize medical marijuana and decriminalize non-medical possession. Teens are going to do something, so why not allow them to purchase the safest drug out there, without risking arrests that could ruin their lives, by chopping away at education and employment opportunities?

Speaking of unsafe drugs: Johnston, the study, the House of Representatives, and the DEA, have not dedicated to prescription pill abuse the same time and conversation they have allotted to these synthetic drugs, because prohibition is not an option.

The Abuse of Prescription Pills

"While the misuse of prescription drugs remains a very important part of the picture," Johnston said, in one hell of a euphemism, "at least their use seems no longer to be growing among teens, and some are declining in use." The report also acknowledges the Food and Drug Administration's coordination with state and local agencies to conduct a "take-back program" to get rid of extra pills, as if hardcore addicts not medically prescribed are getting high every day off their friends' left overs instead of buying them on the street or from a corrupt doctor—and, perhaps more naive—as if taking away a pill eliminates addiction to opioids, the key ingredient in heroin.

Availability itself is clearly not a sole determinant in teens' substance use, as the study itself suggested. Like all fife decisions, associated risk, or whether one expects the act to be harmful, is a huge factor. Thus, when teens are told that if they do LSD, they will stare at the sun until they lose their vision, or that cocaine will make their hearts explode, but their friends report positive experiences with these drugs, they lose trust in the people supposed to educate them on how to safely navigate a society filled with drugs. The result is that they get their information elsewhere; sometimes, it may be beneficial; other times, not so much.

According to the study, 15.2 percent of 12th graders abused prescription pills in the past year, making them the second most commonly used drug behind marijuana—again. Also according to the report, Vicodin use has gone down, but 8% of 12th grades still used in the past year. What's more, nearly 5% of 12th graders used OxyContin, the pill equivalent of heroin, in the past 12 months. Similar numbers report using sedatives, tranquilizers, and Adderall [amphetamines]. Data was not available for perceived risk of opioids, but because more teens reported using these pills than heroin, they, having grown up in a culture of prescription pills, must perceive them to be less threatening.

Unfortunately, prescription pills kill more people than heroin, cocaine, and methamphetamine combined. How is this not the foremost topic of every drug-related conversation?

The Effects of "Generational Forgetting"

The study does not acknowledge a lack of good drug information or harm reduction resources. Instead, it blames "generational forgetting" for older drugs reappearing after their harms have become known and newer drugs increased in popularity.

"There may well be a generational forgetting of the dangers of ecstasy as newer cohorts of youth enter adolescence," comments Johnston. "Because they were quite young when the original ecstasy epidemic occurred, they have had less chance to hear the warnings about the dangers of the drug than did their predecessors."

The study recommended shrinking the time between a drug's emergence and awareness of its negative effects, but the smarter route would be to avoid the harmful effects altogether. Why not take a health-centered approach to these drugs, so that teens may learn how to use them safely, without "generational forgetfulness" kicking in once the government is cracking down on some drug, thus pushing teens towards another one?

Perhaps, if youths received honest drug education in schools, they would not be using prescription pills at rates so high that painkillers, often mixed with anti-anxiety meds and alcohol, have pushed overdose to become the leading cause of accidental death in America.

> "An individual legally enjoys nearly all other rights of adulthood upon turning 18. . . . It is time to reduce the drinking age for all Americans."

The Minimum Legal Drinking Age Should Be Lowered

Michelle Minton

In the following viewpoint, Michelle Minton contends that the current minimum legal drinking age of twenty-one is discriminatory and counterproductive, and leads to widespread disrespect for the law. She argues that the drinking age of twenty-one pushes drinking underground where dangerous and unhealthy practices such as binge drinking predominate. Minton compares US practices to those of European countries where a lower drinking age has not led to harmful results. Minton is the director of insurance studies at the Competitive Enterprise Institute.

As you read, consider the following questions:

1. According to the viewpoint, what percent of graduating high school seniors have broken the law by consuming alcohol?

2. In the viewpoint, the author contends that the drinking age of twenty-one promotes what unhealthy activity?

3. The viewpoint argues that the reduction in traffic fatalities since the establishment of the drinking age of twenty-one is actually more accurately attributed to what factors?

Alaska state representative Bob Lynn (R., Anchorage) is asking the long overdue question: Why do we consider 18-year-olds old enough to join the military, to fight and die for our country, but not to have a drink with their friends before they ship out or while they're home on leave? Lynn has introduced a bill [in March 2011] that would allow anyone 18 years and older with a military ID to drink alcohol in Alaska.

The bill is already facing strong opposition from self-styled public-health advocates. However, the data indicate that the 21-minimum drinking age has not only done zero good, it may actually have done harm. In addition, an individual legally enjoys nearly all other rights of adulthood upon turning 18—including the rights to vote, get married, and sign contracts. It is time to reduce the drinking age for all Americans.

How Twenty-One Became the Legal Drinking Age

In the early 1970s, with the passage of the 26th amendment (which lowered the voting age to 18), 29 states lowered their minimum legal drinking age to 18, 19, or 20 years old. Other states already allowed those as young as 18 to buy alcohol, such as Louisiana, New York, and Colorado. However, after some reports showed an increase in teenage traffic fatalities, some advocacy groups pushed for a higher drinking age. They eventually gained passage of the 1984 National Minimum Drinking Age Act, which lets Congress withhold 10 percent of a state's federal highway funds if it sets its minimum legal drinking age below 21. (Alaska would reportedly lose up to $50 million a year if Lynn's bill passes.)

By 1988, all states had raised their drinking age to 21. In the years since, the idea of lowering the drinking age has periodically returned to the public debate, but groups such as Mothers Against Drunk Driving (MADD) have been able to fight back attempts to change the law. (Louisiana briefly lowered its age limit in back to 18 in 1996, after the state Supreme Court ruled that the 21 limit was a form of age discrimination, but the court reversed that decision a few months later.)

A Culture of Underground Drinking

It's true that America has a problem with drinking: The rates of alcoholism and teenage problem drinking are far greater here than in Europe. Yet in most European countries, the drinking age is far lower than 21. Some, such as Italy, have no drinking age at all. The likely reason for the disparity is the way in which American teens are introduced to alcohol versus their European counterparts. While French or Italian children learn to think of alcohol as part of a meal, American teens learn to drink in the unmonitored environment of a basement or the backwoods with their friends. A 2009 study by the National Institute on Drug Abuse, National Institutes of Health, and U.S. Department of Health and Human Services concluded that 72 percent of graduating high-school seniors had already consumed alcohol.

The problem is even worse on college campuses, where there is an unspoken understanding between students, administrators, local law enforcement, and parents that renders drinking-age restrictions effectively moot as students drink alcohol at frat or house parties and in their dorm rooms. The result is dangerous, secret binge drinking. This unspoken agreement and the problems it creates led a group of college chancellors and presidents from around the nation to form the Amethyst Initiative, which proposes a reconsideration of the current drinking age.

Middlebury College president emeritus John M. McCardell, who is also a charter member of Presidents Against Drunk Driving, came out in favor of lowering the drinking age to

18 years old in a 2004 *New York Times* opinion article. "Our latter-day prohibitionists have driven drinking behind closed doors and underground," he wrote. "Colleges should be given the chance to educate students, who in all other respects are adults, in the appropriate use of alcohol, within campus boundaries and out in the open."

The Link Between Traffic Fatalities and the Drinking Age

The most powerful argument, at least emotionally, for leaving the drinking age at 21 is that the higher age limit has prevented alcohol-related traffic fatalities. Such fatalities indeed decreased about 33 percent from 1988 to 1998—but the trend is not restricted to the United States. In Germany, for example, where the drinking age is 16, alcohol-related fatalities decreased by 57 percent between 1975 and 1990. The most likely cause for the decrease in traffic fatalities is a combination of law enforcement, education, and advances in automobile-safety technologies such as airbags and roll cages.

In addition, statistics indicate that these fatalities may not even have been prevented but rather *displaced* by three years, and that fatalities might even have increased over the long run because of the reduced drinking age. In an award-winning study in 2010, University of Notre Dame undergraduate Dan Dirscherl found that banning the purchase of alcohol between the ages of 18 and 21 actually *increased* traffic fatalities of those between the ages of 18 and 24 by 3 percent. Dirscherl's findings lend credence to the "experienced drinker" hypothesis, which holds that when people begin driving at 16 and gain confidence for five years before they are legally able to drink, they are more likely to overestimate their driving ability and have less understanding of how alcohol consumption affects their ability to drive.

Statistics aside, the drinking age in the U.S. is difficult to enforce and discriminatory toward adults between 18 and 21 years old. The current age limit has created a culture of hidden drinking and disrespect for the law. Regardless of whether an adult is in the military or a civilian, she ought to be treated as just that: an adult. If you are old and responsible enough to go to war, get married, vote, or sign a contract, then you are old and responsible enough to buy a bottle of beer and toast to living in a country that respects and protects individual rights. It is long past time the law caught up with that reality.

*"Alcohol should be forbidden to 18- to
20-year-olds precisely because they
have a propensity to binge drink
whether the stuff is illegal or not."*

The Minimum Legal Drinking Age Should Not Be Lowered

Carla T. Main

*In the following viewpoint, Carla T. Main assesses the arguments
for and against lowering the legal drinking age from the current
age of twenty-one. Main contends that the arguments in favor of
a lower drinking age—especially the argument that binge drinking
would diminish—are simply wrong. She argues that the solution to
the problem of underage drinking is to better enforce the laws that
are currently in place. Main, who produced this policy study for the
Hoover Institute of Stanford University, is the author of* Bulldozed
(2007), and she writes frequently about issues of law and society.

As you read, consider the following questions:

1. Why, according to the author, did many states lower the
   drinking age to eighteen in the early 1970s?
2. What grassroots organization played a big role in getting
   the drinking age moved back up to twenty-one?

3. In the viewpoint, one expert on college drinking believes that what percent of students have "deeply engrained drinking habits" by the time they arrive at college?

The problem of underage drinking on college campuses has been brewing for many years, to the continued vexation of higher education administrators. In 2008, John McCardell, president emeritus of Middlebury College, began to circulate for signature a public statement among colleagues titled "The Amethyst Initiative," which calls for elected officials to reexamine underage drinking laws. The project grew out of outreach efforts of a nonprofit organization he founded in 2007 called Choose Responsibility. The nonprofit advocates lowering the drinking age to 18 and licensing alcohol use for young people in much the same manner as driving—following coursework and an exam. Choose Responsibility also favors the repeal of the laws that set 21 as the mandatory minimum age for drinking (known as the "21 laws") and encourages states at the least to adopt exceptions to the 21 laws that would allow minors to drink at home and in private clubs. It also favors social changes that shift the focus on alcohol use among youth to the home, family, and individual.

The Amethyst Initiative's statement has been signed by 135 college presidents and chancellors at schools from Duke to Bennington. The majority is private; most are in the Northeast. The statement takes no formal position, unlike Choose Responsibility. It does, however, drop heavy hints as to where the debate ought to come out. The statement says "21 is not working" and asks "How many times must we relearn the lessons of Prohibition?" It draws comparisons to other age-of-majority rights conferred on 18-year-olds, such as voting and serving in the military, and calls upon elected officials to consider "whether current public policies are in line with current realities." . . .

Removing the Allure of Drinking

The primary argument made in the Initiative's statement in favor of repealing the 21 laws is that the 21 laws make alcohol taboo, thus driving underage drinking underground and causing more binge drinking to take place than otherwise would, due to the allure of forbidden fruit and the need for secrecy. Hence, by lowering the drinking age, youth consumption would come out in the open and binge drinking would be largely reduced or even eliminated. The second salutary effect of lowering the drinking age, the Initiative argues, would be educational: Colleges would be allowed to have open, frank discussions about responsible drinking. In other words, institutions of higher education could teach young people how to drink responsibly. The Initiative makes vague references to the "unintended consequences" of 21 "posing increasing risks to young people," and says that the original impetus for the 21 laws—reduction of highway fatalities by young drivers—has outlived its usefulness. . . .

The Initiative is a welcome development insofar as it challenges us to examine whether 21 "is working." The answer: It is not, as currently enforced. So should 21 be scrapped or salvaged? First, a look at how we got here, and why the 21 laws are broken. . . .

Raising the Minimum Drinking Age to Twenty-One

During the 19th century, cultural and social norms prevented young people from drinking. The expense and limited availability of liquor also helped keep it out of youthful hands. After Prohibition, it was left up to the states to regulate alcohol, and most states made the legal drinking age 21, the same as the age for voting and other adult rights. The issue remained largely untouched until the late 1960s when protests over the Vietnam War raised the question of the national voting age. For the first time, the question of the draft age and the voting age were linked in the popular imagination, at least among the left. "If a boy is old enough to fight and the for his country, why isn't he old enough to vote?" was the popular refrain.

The legal drinking age got swept up in the political upheaval of the era, as states generally reexamined their age-of-majority laws. Between 1970 and 1976, 29 states lowered their age for drinking alcohol. The results were catastrophic. Highway deaths among teenagers and young adults skyrocketed. Almost immediately, states began raising the minimum drinking age again—years before Congress in 1982 and 1984 dangled the carrot of federal highway monies as an incentive. Between 1976 and 1984, 24 of the 29 states raised the age back up again. By 1984, only three states allowed 18-year-olds to drink. Five states and the District of Columbia regulated various degrees of alcohol consumption among those 18 and over. The remaining states had a patchwork of minimum ages ranging from 19 to 21.

The Link Between the Drinking Age and Drunk Driving

While states experimented with age-of-majority laws, a cultural shift was taking place in how society regarded drunk driving. In 1980, a 13-year-old California girl named Cari Lightner was walking to a carnival when she was struck by a hit-and-run drunk driver and killed instantly. Her mother became enraged when she learned that drunk driving was not treated seriously in the American judicial system. What followed was one of the great stories of American grassroots activism. Together with a friend, Candace Lightner founded Mothers Against Drunk Driving (MADD), which quickly garnered local and later national support in a campaign that focused on putting a human face on the damage done by drunk drivers. By 1982, with MADD 100-chapters strong, President [Ronald] Reagan created a presidential commission to study drunk driving and Congress authorized highway funds to states that passed stiffer drunk driving laws. In 1984, Congress passed the Uniform Drinking Age Act, which required states to have a minimum drinking age of 21 for all types

Underage Drinking Is a Public Health Problem

- Excessive alcohol consumption contributes to more than 4,600 deaths among underage youth, that is, persons less than 21 years of age, in the United States each year.

- Underage drinking is strongly associated with many health and social problems among youth including alcohol-impaired driving, physical fighting, poor school performance, sexual activity, and smoking.

- Most underage youth who drink do so to the point of intoxication, that is, they binge drink (defined as having five or more drinks in a row), typically on multiple occasions.

- Current drinking during the previous month among persons aged 18 to 20 years declined significantly from 59% in 1985 to 40% in 1991, coincident with states adopting an age 21 minimum legal drinking age, but increased to 47% by 1999.

- The prevalence of current drinking among persons aged 21 to 25 also declined significantly from 70% in 1985 to 56% in 1991, but increased to 60% by 1999.

Centers for Disease Control and Prevention, "Fact Sheets: Age 21 Minimum Legal Drinking Age," July 20, 2010.

of alcohol consumption if they wanted to receive federal highway monies. The legal drinking age has stayed at 21 since then.

In most of the television debates about the Amethyst Initiative, the success or failure of 21 has been primarily linked to the issue of highway deaths, with the debaters arguing fatality statistics to prove whether the 21 laws should be shelved because of the advent of safer cars. But that suggests, wrongly, that the debate largely begins and ends with the question of teenage bodies splattered across the interstates. While drunk driving among underage drinkers remains a problem, unfortunately it is only one of several ways that underage drinking threatens young people. Time has not stood still since 1984. American campuses and drinking patterns have changed, and not for the better.

The Law Does Not Lead to Binge Drinking

The logic of the Initiative is that if we take away the allure of illegality, American youth will stop binging. That conclusion is wrong. Alcohol should be forbidden to 18- to 20-year-olds precisely because they have a propensity to binge drink whether the stuff is illegal or not—especially males.

Henry Wechsler and Toben F. Nelson, in the landmark Harvard School of Public Health College Alcohol Study, or CAS, which tracked college student drinking patterns from 1992 to 2001, explained that binge drinking is five or more drinks on one occasion. Binge drinking brings the blood alcohol concentration to 0.08 gram percent or above (typically five drinks for a man or four for a woman within two hours). To understand just how drunk that makes a person, consider that it violates criminal laws to drive with a blood alcohol level of 0.08 gram percent or above.

To call alcohol taboo implies that drinking is done in secret and rarely. Yet college drinking is so common as to have lost all tinge of intrigue. Drinking greases the social wheels, and college life for many is saturated with popular drinking games that no doubt seem brilliant to the late-adolescent: Beerchesi, Beergammon, BeerSoftball, coin games like Psycho, Quarters, and BeerBattleship, and card and dice games linked to beer.

When undergraduates binge drink, they get into trouble—a lot of it. They endanger and sometimes kill their fellow students by setting fires. They sexually assault their female companions (approximately 100,000 incidents annually). They get into fights with other young undergrads (some 700,000 assaults annually). On average 1,100 a year die from alcohol-related traffic crashes and another 300 die in non-traffic alcohol-related deaths. According to the CAS, among the 8 million college students in the United States surveyed in one study year, more than 2 million drove under the influence of alcohol and more than 3 million rode in cars with drivers who had been drinking. Eight percent of students—474,000—have unprotected consensual sex each year because they have been drinking. In short, college students do stupid, illegal, dangerous, and sometimes deadly things when they drink.

Students Bring Drinking Habits to College

Moreover, the drinking doesn't begin in college. More kids drink alcohol than smoke pot, which is the most commonly used illicit drug. A third of our youth taste their first drink before the age of 13 and have drinking patterns as early as 8th to 10th grade. In a pattern that continues in college, boys fall into binge drinking patterns in greater numbers than girls by 12th grade. The Pacific Institute for Research and Evaluation has estimated the social cost of underage drinking (for all youth) at some $53 billion. That includes only highway deaths and injuries and does not factor in brain damage associated with early adolescent drinking, or the array of other injuries and social problems such as opportunity costs that crop up when children drink.

The majority of those who binge drink in college started down that road long before they matriculated—they simply continue their drinking habits once they arrive on campus. Brett Sokolow, president of the consulting firm National Center for Higher Education Risk Management, which counsels colleges on reducing "risk" through educational programs and institutional policies, said in an interview that based on his anecdotal experience, 60 to 70 percent of the students attending his on-campus alcohol seminars have had drinking experiences prior to attending college and about 40 percent have "deeply engrained drinking habits" by the time they get to college. . . .

Enforcing the Law

The Amethyst Initiative says, in essence, that the phenomenon of underage drinking is a tidal wave that society cannot stop. Our only hope is to ride the wave along with our children, give them an oar, and hope they don't drown. That relies on the very big—and untested—assumption that their young minds have the capacity to listen when it comes to alcohol, no matter how badly they want to party, hook up, fit in.

Given the stakes, America should not throw in the towel on the 21 laws until we have actually enforced them as they were meant to be enforced though it will require a clear dedication of political will. It can be done; a similar revolution occurred during the 1980s with respect to driving under the influence laws. Disparities in enforcement do not mean that the laws are impossible to enforce. It signals that we have not gotten serious as a nation about using the laws we have—and improving them where needed.

Periodical and Internet Sources Bibliography

The following articles have been chosen to supplement the diverse views presented in this chapter.

The American Cancer Society	"Child and Teen Tobacco Use: Understanding the Problem," November 10, 2011. www.cancer.org.
Steve Elliott	"Federal Report: Most in Pot Rehab Were Forced Into It," May 28, 2010. www.tokeofthetown.com.
David J. Hanson	"Underage Drinking," 2011. www2.potsdam.edu.
David J. Hanson	"Underage Drinking Rates," 2011. www2.potsdam.edu.
Huffington Post	"Marijuana Use and Driving Under the Influence on the Rise Among Teens, Study Says," February 23, 2012. www.huffingtonpost.com.
Mothers Against Drunk Driving	"Myths and Facts About the 21 Minimum Drinking Age," www.madd.org.
National Institute on Drug Abuse	"Marijuana: Facts for Teens," 2011. www.drugabuse.gov.
National Youth Anti-Drug Media Campaign	"Marijuana Facts," 2011. www.theantidrug.com.
Karen O'Keefe and Mitch Earleywine	"The Impact of State Medical Marijuana Laws," The Marijuana Policy Project, June 2011. www.mpp.org.
Philip Smith	"Teens Rejecting Alcohol, Tobacco; Selecting Marijuana," December 14, 2011. www.stopthedrugwar.org.
Michael Winerip	"High Season: Teens and Marijuana Use," *Family Circle*, 2012. www.familycircle.com.

OPPOSING
VIEWPOINTS®
SERIES

CHAPTER 3

Does Sexuality Put Teens at Risk?

Chapter Preface

Teens today are bombarded with images of teen sex from all directions, especially in popular media. Reality TV shows such as *Teen Mom* and *16 and Pregnant* depict teen moms struggling with adult roles and responsibilities. Some say these shows indirectly glorify teenage mothers—and single mothers—while others say these shows help deter teenage girls from getting pregnant. In any case, a February 2012 report by the Guttmacher Institute revealed that the teenage pregnancy rate has declined to its lowest rate since 1972. In direct correlation, the teenage rate of abortions has also declined to its lowest rate since statistics have been kept, to 17.8 per 1,000 teenage girls.

While most observers celebrate these positive trends, the details can still be quite sobering. Though abortion rates have fallen, one in ten girls will still get an abortion by the age of twenty. Also, abortion rates for Hispanic and African American girls have fallen, but not nearly as much as rates for white girls. Abortion rates for Hispanic girls are still twice as high as those for white girls, and rates for African American girls are four times as high.

What are the factors behind this decrease in abortion rates? Demographer Kathryn Kost, one of the authors of the Guttmacher report, says that most of the credit for this decline goes to increased and more effective use of contraception. As the report notes: "Among women age 15–17, about one-quarter of the decline was attributed to reduced sexual activity and three-quarters to increased contraceptive use." The Guttmacher Institute is a reproductive health non-profit organization that promotes contraception and supports abortion rights. The Centers for Disease Control echoes Kost's conclusion but adds that the economic recession has also played a significant role in the recent decline in teen pregnancies and abortions in the United States.

In contrast, Kristan Hawkins, writing for the pro-life news agency LifeNews, argues that abstinence sex education should receive some credit for the downturn in teen pregnancy and abortions. Further, statistics on teen use of the emergency contraception (Plan B), which has only been available since 2006, are not available. So the role of the morning after pill in reducing teen pregnancy and abortions is not known. Hawkins concludes that it is too soon to draw definite conclusions: "What is really causing the decline in teen birth rates? The economy, school based contraception or abstinence based sex education, or cheap over the counter emergency contraception? We really don't know." Teen abortion and pregnancy rates are among the issues debated in the following chapter.

> *"Too often, the more comfortable term*
> *bullying is used to describe sexual*
> *harassment, obscuring the role of*
> *gender and sex in these incidents."*

Sexual Harassment Pervasive in US Middle and High Schools, Survey Finds

David Crary

The following viewpoint assesses the results of a recent nationwide survey on sexual harassment in grades seven through twelve. The survey reveals the negative impact of sexual harassment on teens, and it notes how few incidents are actually reported by victims to school authorities. Though in some cases bullying and sexual harassment overlap, it is important to understand the difference. The author, David Crary, writes for the Associated Press and the Huffington Post.

As you read, consider the following questions:

1. According to the survey cited in the viewpoint, what percent of students in grades seven through twelve experienced some form of sexual harassment in the 2010–2011 school year?

2. What percentage of harassed students ends up reporting the incident to a teacher, counselor, or other adult at the school, according to the viewpoint?
3. According to the viewpoint, what is the purpose of most harassing remarks made by students?

It can be a malicious rumor whispered in the hallway, a lewd photo arriving by cell phone, hands groping where they shouldn't. Added up, it's an epidemic—student-on-student sexual harassment that is pervasive in America's middle schools and high schools.

During the 2010–2011 school year, 48 percent of students in grades seventh through twelfth experienced some form of sexual harassment in person or electronically via texting, email and social media, according to a major national survey being released Monday by the American Association of University Women.

The harassers often thought they were being funny, but the consequences for their targets can be wrenching, according to the survey. Nearly a third of the victims said the harassment made them feel sick to their stomach, affected their study habits or fueled reluctance to go to school at all.

"It's reached a level where it's almost a normal part of the school day," said one of the report's co-authors, AAUW director of research Catherine Hill. "It's somewhat of a vicious cycle. The kids who are harassers often have been harassed themselves."

The survey, conducted in May and June, asked 1,002 girls and 963 boys from public and private schools nationwide whether they had experienced any of various forms of sexual harassment. These included having someone make unwelcome sexual comments about them, being called gay or lesbian in a negative way, being touched in an unwelcome sexual way, being shown sexual pictures they didn't want to see, and being the subject of unwelcome sexual rumors.

The survey quoted one ninth-grade girl as saying she was called a whore "because I have many friends that are boys." A 12th-grade boy said schoolmates circulated an image showing his face attached to an animal having sex.

In all, 56 percent of the girls and 40 percent of the boys said they had experienced at least one incident of sexual harassment during the school year.

After being harassed, half of the targeted students did nothing about it. Of the rest, some talked to parents or friends, but only 9 percent reported the incident to a teacher, guidance counselor or other adult at school, according to the survey.

Reasons for not reporting included doubts it would have any impact, fears of making the situation worse, and concerns about the staff member's reaction.

The report comes at a time when the problem of bullying at schools is in the spotlight, in part because of several recent suicides of beleaguered students.

The AAUW report observes that sexual harassment and bullying can sometimes overlap, such as the taunting of youths who are perceived to be gay or lesbian, but it says there are important distinctions. For example, there are some state laws against bullying, but serious sexual harassment—at a level which interferes with a student's education—is prohibited under the federal gender-equality legislation known as Title IX.

"Too often, the more comfortable term bullying is used to describe sexual harassment, obscuring the role of gender and sex in these incidents," the report says. "Schools are likely to promote bullying prevention while ignoring or downplaying sexual harassment."

Fatima Goss Graves, a vice president of the National Women's Law Center in Washington, said the ultimate goal should be to deter hurtful student interactions however they are defined.

"Schools get too caught up in the label," she said. "If it's the sort of conduct that's interfering with a student's performance, it ought to be stopped."

The survey asked students for suggestions on how to reduce sexual harassment at their schools. More than half favored systematic punishments for harassers and said there should be a mechanism for reporting harassment anonymously.

The AAUW report said all schools should create a sexual-harassment policy and make sure it is publicized and enforced. It said schools must ensure that students are educated about what their rights are under Title IX, with special attention paid to encouraging girls to respond assertively to harassment since they are targeted more often than boys.

Niobe Way, a professor of applied psychology at New York University who has studied adolescent relationships, suggested that school anti-harassment policies might have only limited impact without broader cultural changes that break down gender stereotypes.

"You have a culture that doesn't value boys having close intimate relations and being emotional or empathetic," she said.

Bill Bond, a former high school principal who is a school safety expert for the National Association of Secondary School Principals, said there had been in shift in the nature of sexual harassment among students over recent decades.

"Overt attempts to exploit a fellow student sexually have become less common, while there's more use of sexual remarks to degrade or insult someone," he said.

"Words can cut a kid all the way to the heart," Bond said. "And when it's on the computers and cell phones, there's no escape. It's absolutely devastating and vicious to a kid."

The survey was conducted for AAUW by Knowledge Networks, and students answered the questions online, rather than to a person, to maximize the chances that they would answer sensitive questions candidly.

"The Internet didn't create the turmoil of the teen years and young adulthood— romantic breakups, bitter fights among best friends, jealous rivalries, teasing and bullying. But it does amplify it."

Poll: Young People Say Online Meanness Pervasive

CBS News

The following viewpoint reports that a high percentage of teens have experienced troublesome online behavior such as bullying, harassment, and "sexting." The results of the AP-MTV Poll behind these statistics show that these online problems have gotten worse over the past two years (from 2009 to 2011). For middle and high school students, the victimization rates for cyberbullying are around 20 to 25 percent, the viewpoint argues. Though the practice of "sexting" sexually provocative photos has not increased notably, it still remains high. CBS News is a division of the US television and radio network CBS.

As you read, consider the following questions:

1. According the AP-MTV Poll cited in the viewpoint, what percentage of youth have been the target of online harassment or bullying?

2. Instead of the narrower term "cyberbullying," what broader term is being used to describe these mean online behaviors, according to the viewpoint?
3. Though only 7 percent of teens say they have directly been involved in "sexting," what percent say they have been exposed to it?

Catherine Devine had her first brush with an online bully in seventh grade, before she'd even ventured onto the Internet. Someone set up the screen name "devinegirl" and, posing as Catherine, sent her classmates instant messages full of trashy talk and lies. "They were making things up about me, and I was the most innocent 12-year-old ever," Devine remembers. "I hadn't even kissed anybody yet."

As she grew up, Devine, now 22, learned to thrive in the electronic village. But like other young people, she occasionally stumbled into one of its dark alleys.

A new Associated Press-MTV poll of youth in their teens and early 20s finds that most of them—56 percent—have been the target of some type of online taunting, harassment or bullying, a slight increase over just two years ago. A third say they've been involved in "sexting," the sharing of naked photos or videos of sexual activity. Among those in a relationship, 4 out of 10 say their partners have used computers or cellphones to abuse or control them.

Three-fourths of the young people said they consider these darker aspects of the online world, sometimes broadly called "digital abuse," a serious problem.

They're not the only ones.

President Barack Obama brought students, parents and experts together at the White House in March to try to confront "cyberbullying." The Education Department sponsors an annual conference to help schools deal with it. Teen suicides linked to vicious online bullying have caused increasing worry in communities across the country.

Conduct that rises to the point of bullying is hard to define, but the AP-MTV poll of youth ages 14 to 24 showed plenty of rotten behavior online, and a perception that it's increasing. The share of young people who frequently see people being mean to each other on social networking sites jumped to 55 percent, from 45 percent in 2009.

That may be partly because young people are spending more time than ever communicating electronically: 7 in 10 had logged into a social networking site in the previous week, and 8 in 10 had texted a friend.

"The Internet is an awesome resource," says Devine, "but sometimes it can be really negative and make things so much worse."

Devine, who lives on New York's Long Island, experienced her share of online drama in high school and college: A friend passed around highly personal entries from Devine's private electronic journal when she was 15. She left her Facebook account open on a University of Scranton library computer, and a prankster posted that she was pregnant (she wasn't). Most upsetting, when she was 18, Devine succumbed to a boyfriend's pressure to send a revealing photo of herself, and when they broke up he briefly raised the threat of embarrassing her with it.

"I didn't realize the power he could have over me from that," Devine said. "I thought he'd just see it once and then delete it, like I had deleted it."

The Internet didn't create the turmoil of the teen years and young adulthood—romantic breakups, bitter fights among best friends, jealous rivalries, teasing and bullying. But it does amplify it. Hurtful words that might have been shouted in the cafeteria, within earshot of a dozen people, now can be blasted to hundreds on Facebook.

"It's worse online, because everybody sees it," said Tiffany Lyons, 24, of Layton, Utah. "And once anything gets online you can't get rid of it."

Plus, 75 percent of youth think people do or say things online that they wouldn't do or say face to face.

The most common complaints were people spreading false rumors on Internet pages or by text message, or being downright mean online; more than a fifth of young people said each of those things had happened to them. Twenty percent saw someone take their electronic messages and share them without permission, and 16 percent said someone posted embarrassing pictures or video of them without their permission.

Some of these are one-time incidents; others cross into repeated harassment or bullying.

Sameer Hinduja, a cyberbullying researcher, said numerous recent studies taken together suggest a cyberbullying victimization rate of 20 to 25 percent for middle and high school students. Many of these same victims also suffer from in-person abuse. Likewise, many online aggressors are also real-world bullies.

"We are seeing offenders who are just jerks to people online and offline," said Hinduja, an associate professor of criminal justice at Florida Atlantic University and co-director of the Cyberbullying Research Center.

And computers and cellphones increase the reach of old-fashioned bullying.

"When I was bullied in middle school I could go home and slam my door and forget about it for a while," said Hinduja. "These kids can be accessed around the clock through technology. There's really no escape."

"Sexting," or sending nude or sexual images, is more common among those over 18 than among minors. And it hasn't shown much increase in the past two years. Perhaps young people are thinking twice before hitting "send" after publicity about adults—even members of Congress—losing their jobs over sexual images, and news stories of young teens risking child pornography charges if they're caught.

Fifteen percent of young people had shared a nude photo of themselves in some way or another; that stood at 7 percent among teens and 19 percent among young adults. But almost a

Website Bullying

Beneath a heading that read "She's queer because," students posted their own crude epithets about eighth grader Kylie Kenney. The website—called *Kill Kylie Incorporated*—had been set up by some of her fellow students. Kylie learned of it only when a classmate asked if she had seen the website. She hadn't, nor could she understand why someone would do such a thing.

Beginning with the day the website was set up, Kylie endured two years of relentless cyber- and face-to-face bullying from classmates. "I had no escape," she said later. "Everything followed me to school." It got to the point where these mean kids used Kylie's screen name to pretend to be her online and make sexually suggestive remarks about Kylie's teammates on the field hockey team. They even asked her teammates out on dates, posing as Kylie all the while. Nine months later, the students behind the website were finally discovered. Two students were suspended, and the police filed charges of harassment against one person who had made a death threat online against Kylie.

This is but one variety of the most popular strategy among tech-savvy bullies: directly attacking the victim through the Internet while remaining completely anonymous.

Edward F. Dragan, The Bully Action Guide. *New York: Palgrave Macmillan, 2011, p. 182.*

fourth of the younger group said they'd been exposed to sexting in some way, including seeing images someone else was showing around. And 37 percent of the young adults had some experience with "sexting" images.

Many young people don't take sexting seriously, despite the potential consequences.

Alec Wilhelmi, 20, says girlfriends and girls who like him have sent sexual messages or pictures—usually photos of bare body parts that avoid showing faces. Once a friend made a sexual video with his girlfriend, and showed Wilhelmi on his cellphone.

"I thought that was funny, because I don't know what kind of girl would allow that," said Wilhelmi, a freshman at Iowa State University.

Technology can facilitate dating abuse. Nearly 3 in 10 young people say their partner has checked up on them electronically multiple times per day or read their text messages without permission. Fourteen percent say they've experienced more abusive behavior from their partners, such as name-calling and mean messages via Internet or cellphone.

The AP-MTV poll was conducted Aug. 18–31 and involved online interviews with 1,355 people ages 14–24 nationwide. . . .

The poll is part of an MTV campaign, "A Thin Line," aiming to stop the spread of digital abuse.

> *"Programs that teach sexual abstinence until marriage . . . assist adolescents in establishing positive character traits, formulating long-term goals, and developing emotionally healthy relationships."*

Teen Sex Education Should Emphasize Abstinence Until Marriage

Alean Zeiler

The following viewpoint describes the risks faced by sexually active teens—risks that include the possibility of acquiring a sexually transmitted infection (STI) or becoming pregnant. Comprehensive sex education has taught methods of safe sex, but these are not 100 percent safe and effective in preventing infection or pregnancy according to the viewpoint. For this reason the American College of Pediatricians endorses only sex education programs that teach abstinence until marriage. Alean Zeiler is a member of the American College of Pediatricians, a socially conservative organization of about two hundred pediatricians and health care professionals who broke away from the sixty thousand-member American Academy of Pediatricians in 2002.

As you read, consider the following questions:

1. What percentage of sexually active female adolescents has been infected with a sexually transmitted infection (STI), according to the viewpoint?

2. The viewpoint endorses the position of researcher Jay Giedd who argues that young people do not have the capacity to make fully mature decisions until what age?

3. According to the viewpoint, what percentage of adults and teens agree that teens should hear a strong abstinence message?

By every measure, adolescent sexual activity is detrimental to the well-being of all involved, especially young women, and society at large. Children and adolescents from 10 to 19 years of age are more at risk for contracting a sexually transmitted infection (STI) than adults. This is due to the general practice of having multiple and higher risk sexual partners, and to the immaturity of the cervical tissue of girls and young women. The CDC [Centers for Disease Control and Prevention] recently stated that of the 19 million new cases of STIs annually reported in the United States, 50 percent occur in teens and young adults under 25 years of age. Twenty-five percent of newly diagnosed cases of HIV occur in those under 22 years of age. This translates into one in four sexually active female adolescents being infected with at least one STI.

The Risk of Disease and Pregnancy

Bacterial STIs may cause life-threatening cases of pelvic inflammatory disease (PID) and infertility. Viral STIs which include herpes, the Human Papilloma Virus (HPV) and HIV are generally incurable. Herpes afflicts its victims with life-long painful recurrences, may be passed on to sexual partners even when asymptomatic, and may be life threatening to infants if passed on at birth during vaginal delivery. HPV is found among 90 percent of sexually active young adults and teens. While often self-limited, HPV has high-risk strains that may persist for life and cause cancer of the cervix. HIV not only causes premature demise, but also significant suffering with life-long dependence on multiple toxic and costly medications. The CDC estimates that STIs cost the U.S. health care system as much as $15.3 billion dollars annually.

Adolescent pregnancy is similarly associated with adverse socioeconomics that have an impact on the family, community, and society at large. One in thirteen high school girls becomes pregnant each year. Adolescent pregnancy results in decreased educational and vocational opportunities for the mothers, an increased likelihood of the family living in poverty, and significant risk for negative long-term outcomes for the children. For example, children of adolescent mothers are more likely to be born prematurely and at a low birth weight; suffer from poor health; perform poorly in school; run away from home; be abused or neglected; and grow up without a father.

The Link Between Sexual Activity and Emotional Trauma

Even if sexually active teens escape acquiring sexually transmitted infections (STIs) and becoming pregnant, few remain emotionally unscathed. Overall, one in eight teens suffers from depression, and suicide has risen to become the third leading cause of death for adolescents, paralleling the rise in STIs within this population. Infection with an STI has long been recognized as a cause for depression among teens. More recently, however, adolescent sexual activity alone has been acknowledged as an independent risk factor for developing low self-esteem, major depression, and attempting suicide. In studies that controlled for confounding factors, sexually active girls were found to be three times as likely to report being depressed and three times as likely to have attempted suicide when compared to sexually abstinent girls. Sexually active boys were more than twice as likely to suffer from depression and seven times as likely to have attempted suicide when compared to sexually abstinent boys. This is not mere coincidence. Scientists now know that sexual activity releases chemicals in the brain that create emotional bonds between partners. Breaking these bonds can cause depression, and make it harder to bond with someone else in the future.

Sexual activity is defined as genital contact. This includes mutual masturbation, as well as oral, vaginal, and anal intercourse. While only vaginal intercourse may result in pregnancy, all of these practices may spread STIs, and lead to emotional trauma. Abstaining from all sexual activity is the only 100 percent safe and effective way to avoid teen pregnancies, STIs, and the emotional fallout of adolescent sexual activity. Almost 40 years of emphasis on "safer sex" with "values-neutral sex education," condoms and contraception has clearly failed our young people. Abstinence education does not occur in a vacuum, making it especially difficult to separate its influence from the opposing influence of the media and cultural milieu. Nevertheless, effectiveness of abstinence sex education in delaying the onset of sexual debut has been demonstrated in rigorous scientific studies. For example, five out of seven programs recently reviewed showed a significant reduction in sexual initiation rates (two programs showed rates decreased by half). Evaluation of community-based abstinence programs in peer-reviewed journals showed that they are effective in significantly reducing pregnancy. According to an April 2008 report by the Heritage Foundation "fifteen studies examined abstinence programs and eleven reported positive findings of delayed sexual initiation." . . . These do not begin to thoroughly evaluate the hundreds of ongoing programs.

The Two Approaches to Sex Education

In its endorsement of abstinence-based sex education, the [American College of Pediatricians] calls attention to the scientific controversies surrounding alternative educational platforms. Most sex education curricula fall into two categories, *abstinence-until-marriage* or *comprehensive sex education pro-*

grams (occasionally also referred to as "abstinence plus" programs). Recently, abstinence education has been criticized for not providing critical health information about condom use. Abstinence education curricula, however, do not discourage the use of condoms; rather they note that chastity obviates the need for condoms. Abstinence education programs do not claim that condoms have no place in preventing STIs. Comprehensive programs, on the other hand, are misleading in the emphasis they place on condom use. These programs give teens the impression that condoms make sexual activity safe. In reality, there has been much conflicting medical literature on the effectiveness of condoms in preventing STIs since the 2000 NIH report on the subject and much of the controversy remains unresolved. Teens must be informed that condoms do not offer complete protection from either pregnancy or STIs.

The [American College of Pediatricians] position supporting abstinence-until-marriage education, unlike alternative education platforms, also recognizes the unique neurobiology of adolescent brains. The frontal cortex of the adolescent brain is still in development and unable to make the consistently wise executive decisions necessary to control action based on emotional input. Researcher Jay Giedd and others have found that young people do not have the physical brain capacity to make fully mature decisions until their mid-twenties.

The Role of Parents in Sex Education

Consequently, when it comes to sex education, adolescents need to be given clear direction repeatedly, as is done with programs that address smoking, drugs, and alcohol use. Emphasis on contraceptive methods undermines the authority of parents and the strength of the abstinence message. This approach reinforces the ubiquitous (yet erroneous) message presented by the media that engaging in sexual activity is not only expected of teens, but also the norm. Adolescent brains are not equipped to handle these mixed messages. Parents and teachers need to

Choosing Abstinence

In general, I think the debate over abstinence would benefit by being depoliticized. Let's separate the merit of different abstinence programs from whether it's acceptable for teens to choose abstinence for themselves. Teenagers are looking for more than just "the facts"; they also need a positive goal to aspire to. The best abstinence programs do cover this, but even if they don't, that doesn't mean it's wrong for individual students to choose to postpone sex. Too often, those who oppose abstinence education and call it "ignorance-only education" end up sounding as if they oppose the actual choice to postpone—that choice is "unrealistic," they will often say. I think this is a destructive message, because when teens sit down to make their choices, the table is already set for them with the expectation that they are going to have sex right this minute. In spite of all the talk to the contrary, teens who pledge abstinence are less likely to engage in risky sexual behavior than non-pledgers (and pledgers are also less likely to have children out of wedlock, to have sex before age eighteen, and to have extramarital affairs as adults). So individual abstinence commitments are something I think everyone can support, even if he or she is opposed to particular curriculums.

Wendy Shalit, Girls Gone Mild. *New York: Random House, 2007, p. 60.*

"function as a surrogate set of frontal lobes, an auxiliary problem solver" for their teens, setting firm and immutable expectations. Adolescents need repetitive, clear, and consistent guidance.

As families address this issue of sex education, the American College of Pediatricians recommends that parents be fully aware of the content of the curriculum to which their children are being exposed. The national "Guidelines for Comprehensive Sex Education" that were drafted by the Sexuality Information and Education Council of the United States (SIECUS) place strong emphasis on "values neutral" sex education beginning in *kindergarten*. According to these guidelines, children between the ages of 5 to 8 should be taught not only the anatomically correct names of all body parts, but also the definitions of sexual intercourse, and masturbation.

The Problem with Comprehensive Programs

Overall, these comprehensive programs only emphasize "safer sex." Many comprehensive programs also provide sexually erotic material to teens with explicit condom demonstrations. Other programs suggest alternative types of sexually stimulating contact (referred to as "outercourse") that would not result in pregnancy but still could result in STIs. Some of these activities, depending on the ages of those involved and the state in which they occur, could actually be illegal. These education programs can break down the natural barriers of those not yet involved in sexual activity and encourage experimentation. Additionally, many programs emphasize that teens do not need parental consent to obtain birth control and that teens therefore need not even discuss the issue with them.

Discouraging parental involvement eliminates one of the most powerful deterrents to sexual activity, namely, communication of parental expectations. Firm statements from parents that sex should be reserved for marriage have been found to be very effective in delaying sexual debut. Parental example and "religiosity" have also been found to be similarly protective. Adolescents reared by parents who live according to their professed faith and are actively involved in their worship community, are more likely to abstain from sexual activity as teens. Successful sex education programs involve parents and promote open discussion between parents and their children.

The Role of Government in Sex Education

The American College of Pediatricians also believes parents should be aware of the current state of funding, and government involvement in sex education choices. Comprehensive programs receive seven to twelve times the funding of abstinence programs. However, according to a recent study by the Department of Health and Human Services, comprehensive programs do not give equal time to abstinence.

In 2004 Congressman Henry Waxman of California presented a report before Congress critical of the medical accuracy of abstinence education curricula. The Mathematica Study was similarly critical of the medical accuracy of abstinence education programs. However, in 2007 the U.S. Department of Health and Human Services conducted an extensive review of nine comprehensive sex education curricula using the same methods employed by Congressman Waxman and the Mathematica Study. These comprehensive programs were found to have no better record for medical accuracy. The HHS review also found that the comprehensive programs were hardly comprehensive. The amount of discussion dedicated to "safer sex" exceeded that spent on abstinence by a factor of up to seven. Some of the programs failed to mention abstinence altogether. None of the programs carefully distinguished between reducing and eliminating the risks of sexual activity, and nearly every program failed to mention the emotional consequences of early sexual activity. Although some of the comprehensive programs showed a small effect in reducing "unprotected" sex (7 of 9 programs) and to a lesser extent in delaying sexual debut (2 of 8 programs), the impact did not extend beyond six months.

According to a 2004 Zogby Poll, 90% of adults and teens agree with The American College of Pediatricians position that teens should be given a strong abstinence message. Programs that teach sexual abstinence until marriage are about much more than simply delaying sexual activity. They assist adolescents in establishing positive character traits, formulating long-term goals, and developing emotionally healthy relationships. These programs increase the likelihood of strong marriages and families—the single most essential resource for the strength and survival of our nation.

"*The need to support comprehensive sex education over abstinence . . . programs should not be about political gamesmanship or the culture wars, although, too often, it appears that it is.*"

Teen Sex Education Should Emphasize Protection and Safety

Patrick Malone and Monica Rodriguez

The following viewpoint evaluates the two main competing approaches to teaching sex education in the United States: the comprehensive approach and the approach called abstinence until marriage. The authors contend that the emphasis on abstinence programs since the mid-1990s has not been productive. Citing two landmark studies from the year 2007, the authors argue that comprehensive sex education, which emphasizes protection and safety, is much more effective than abstinence until marriage education. Patrick Malone is the director of communications for the Sexuality Information and Education Council of the United States (SIECUS), and Monica Rodriguez is president and CEO of SIECUS.

As you read, consider the following questions:

1. Modern sex education took shape as a response to what health epidemic of the 1980s, according to the authors?
2. According to the viewpoint, abstinence education teaches that the only proper sexual activity is within opposite sex marriage. Which group of students is left out by this approach?
3. The issue of "medical accuracy" is addressed in the viewpoint by focusing on what claim by those who teach abstinence education?

Everyone has an opinion about sexuality education. From vocal parents at PTA meetings to state governors who must decide whether to apply for federal funding for abstinence-only-until-marriage programs or more comprehensive sexuality programs, or both, or neither. From school principals who have to choose which sex education speakers to let into their schools to presidential candidates who have to defend their views from the most zealot activists.

Culture Wars and Sex Education

Add into this mixture the $1.5 billion that was funneled by the federal government to the abstinence-only-until-marriage industry between 1996 and 2009 and you have a volatile concoction indeed. With so much money at stake, and with such differing moral and ethical views of how to approach it, sexuality education has, in many ways, taken over from abortion as the leading symbolic fight in the culture wars. This conflict has led to fights over laws, policies, and implementation on every level—federal, state, and local—that still rage across the country today.

Much of this conflict can trace its roots to the beginning of the modern era of sex education, which began, roughly, around the time that the HIV/AIDS epidemic entered the national spotlight in the late 1980s and early 1990s. Almost as quickly as there were curricula teaching that condoms were extremely effective in combating the spread of HIV, other curricula were introduced that denigrated condoms' effectiveness, comparing using a condom to playing Russian roulette and blaming "victims" of HIV/AIDS for their own complicity in contracting what was then viewed by many as a primarily homosexual disease.

During the second half of the 1990s and most of the 2000s, as the religious right ascended in power and influence, so too did the groups that were fighting what was, for them, essentially an anti-condom campaign. And although the right wing bears most of the responsibility for the push against comprehensive sexuality education, it was actually in 1996, under President Bill Clinton, that the abstinence-only-until-marriage industry scored one of its largest victories when, under Title V Section 510 of the Social Security Act, the federal government started granting $50 million a year to state governments to dole out to sub-grantees to carry out these programs.

The Two Competing Approaches

The argument between supporters of comprehensive sexuality education programs and abstinence-only-until-marriage programs is being fought on two fronts: from an ethical standpoint and from an effectiveness standpoint. From an ethical standpoint, the two arguments are quite distinct.

Comprehensive sexuality education, according to the *Guidelines for Comprehensive Sexuality Education* from the Sexuality Information and Education Council of the United States (SIECUS), "should be appropriate to the age, developmental level, and cultural background of students and respect the diversity of values and beliefs represented in the community. Comprehensive school-based sexuality education complements and augments the sexuality education children receive from their families, religious and community groups, and healthcare professionals." This includes teaching not only about abstinence, but also contraception, including emergency contraception; reproductive choice; lesbian, gay, bisexual, transgender (LGBT), and questioning issues; as well as, of course, anatomy; development; puberty; relationships; and all of the other issues one would expect to be covered in a traditional sexuality education class. Furthermore, comprehensive sexuality education should be science-based and medically accurate.

Supporters of abstinence-only-until-marriage programs, on the other hand, strive to create an environment in which young people are prepared and able to remain abstinent because they believe that abstinence is the only completely effective form of birth control and the only way to completely avoid the risk of sexually transmitted diseases (STDs). (Abstinence is only effective if used consistently and correctly; "abstinent" teens have a comparatively high STD infection rate).

The Narrow Guidelines of Abstinence-Only Programs

Part of Section 510(b) of Title V of the Social Security Act, known as the "A–H guidelines," are the eight criteria that abstinence-only-until-marriage programs had to conform to in order to be eligible to receive federal funding, and they offer insight into the motivations and values of supporters of the programs because many of the supporters of these requirements actually receive funding through the Title V program. They state that an eligible program:

A. Has as its exclusive purpose teaching the social, psychological, and health gains to be realized by abstaining from sexual activity;

B. Teaches abstinence from sexual activity outside marriage as the expected standard for all school-age children;

C. Teaches that abstinence from sexual activity is the only certain way to avoid out-of-wedlock pregnancy, sexually transmitted diseases, and other associated health problems;

D. Teaches that a mutually faithful, monogamous relationship in the context of marriage is the expected standard of sexual activity;

E. Teaches that sexual activity outside the context of marriage is likely to have harmful psychological and physical effects;

F. Teaches that bearing children out of wedlock is likely to have harmful consequences for the child, the child's parents, and society;

G. Teaches young people how to reject sexual advances and how alcohol and drug use increase vulnerability to sexual advances; and

H. Teaches the importance of attaining self-sufficiency before engaging in sexual activity.

Taken together, the A–H guidelines present a very clear view that what is most valued in abstinence-only-until-marriage programs are the ideas that sexual activity inside the context of marriage is the only proper behavior (which, of course, excludes LGBT individuals), and that sexual activity and childrearing outside marriage are likely to have myriad negative personal and societal effects.

Clearly, most people are drawn to one of these approaches over the other based on their personal morals, ethics, politics, or religion. However, just because an educational philosophy reflects an individual's or institution's personal beliefs does not necessarily mean that it is effective. "Effectiveness" has really become the key word in the debate for a few reasons.

First, because teen pregnancy and STD rates are so high in the United States, parents, policymakers, and educators have a compelling interest in finding sexuality education programs that will lower them. Education may be a valued investment per se, but there is now a higher demand to see actual, quantifiable results that show progress in combating teen pregnancy and STDs.

The 'Abstinence Only' Lifeguard

Second, effectiveness is important because of the tightened fiscal situation faced by states and localities across the county. When so little money is available for essential programs, such as fire departments and police, no policymaker wants to be caught funding sex education programs that don't work.

The Findings of Recent Landmark Studies

Fortunately, the answer to whether comprehensive sexuality education or abstinence-only-until-marriage programs are more effective is perfectly clear. Two landmark studies, both released in 2007, conducted broad examinations of abstinence-only-until-marriage programs and comprehensive sexuality education programs. What these studies found is as important as it is unsurprising.

The first study, dealing with abstinence-only-until-marriage programs, "Impacts of Four Title V, Section 510 Abstinence Education Programs," conducted by Mathematica Policy Research,

Inc. on behalf of the U.S. Department of Health and Human Services, focused on four federally funded abstinence-only-until-marriage programs in different communities. The study found no evidence that abstinence-only-until-marriage programs increased rates of sexual abstinence.

In addition, students in the abstinence-only-until-marriage programs had a similar number of sexual partners as their peers in the control group as well as a similar age of first intercourse. Furthermore, participants in both the study and control groups had the same rate of unprotected sexual intercourse. Without delving too far into the methodology of the study, it is important to know that it concentrated on programs that were implemented in elementary and middle schools and followed up with participants four to six years later.

Comprehensive Sex Education Is More Successful

The second study, "Emerging Answers 2007: Research Findings on Programs to Reduce Teen Pregnancy and Sexually Transmitted Diseases," conducted by Douglas Kirby, Ph.D., was a meta-evaluation that reviewed several other studies that had been conducted on the effectiveness of both abstinence-only-until-marriage programs and comprehensive sexuality education to draw broader conclusions and identify trends.

Like the Mathematica study, Kirby's study came to the conclusion that there was no strong evidence that abstinence-only-until-marriage programs delay the initiation of sexual intercourse, hasten the return to abstinence, or reduce the number of sexual partners. The study did find that two-thirds of the comprehensive programs examined had at least one positive sexual behavioral effect. In fact, 40 percent of the comprehensive programs examined achieved the three important effects of delaying the initiation of sexual intercourse, reducing the number of sexual partners, and increasing condom or contraceptive use. For the purposes of this study, abstinence programs were defined as those that encourage and expect young people to remain abstinent, while comprehensive programs are defined as those that "encourage abstinence as the safest choice but also encourage young people who are having sex to always use condoms or other measures of contraception."

Taken in conjunction, the two studies make a strong case that any future investment in school-based sexuality education should be focused on comprehensive sexuality education. While Kirby's study reveals that there can be, and indeed are, shortcomings in some comprehensive programs, the very fact that a substantial majority of them show a positive sexual behavioral effect puts them head and shoulders above abstinence-only-until-marriage programs, which are almost completely ineffective in achieving their stated goals.

The irony of the situation, however, is that those parents and policymakers who most want young people to remain abstinent *still* support abstinence-only-until-marriage programs when they should be supporting comprehensive sexuality education, which holds far more promise for delaying the initiation of sexual activity among young people. . . .

Sex Education Programs Must Be Medically Accurate

While perusing laws and pending legislation mandating comprehensive sexuality education, one would certainly come across the words and phrases "age appropriate," "proven effective," "science-based," "complete," "unbiased," and "medically accurate." All of these are important and should certainly be included in any *ideal* legislation, but, in reality, the most important, and absolutely necessary, is to mandate that sexuality education programs be medically accurate.

The easiest way to explain why medical accuracy is so important is to look at an example from an abstinence-only-until-marriage curriculum. The following is taken from the *Why kNOw Abstinence Education Program Teacher's Manual* published in 2002:

The condom has a 14% failure rate in preventing pregnancy . . . since the HIV virus is smaller than a sperm and can infect you any day of the month, the failure rate of the condom to prevent AIDS is logically much worse than its failure rate to prevent pregnancy.

This is a medically inaccurate statement. The 14 percent failure rate for condoms cited in the first part of the statement is known as the "typical" or "user" failure rate. This means that it includes all people who use condoms, even if they do not use them consistently or correctly. In other words, the 14 percent includes condom users who put a condom on in the middle of intercourse, put a condom on inside out, open the wrapper with their teeth and rip the condom, or simply use a condom every other time they have sex, or less. In reality, the failure rate for male condoms for people who use them consistently and correctly, known as the "method" failure rate, is 2 percent, according to the Centers for Disease Control and Prevention (CDC).

Finally, the logic used in the second half of the statement would be almost laughable were it not so dangerous. All that needs to be said in rebuttal is that, according to the CDC, "laboratory studies have demonstrated that latex condoms provide an essentially impermeable barrier to particles the size of HIV."

This is just one example of how, in a single statement, medical inaccuracies can grossly distort the truth about what could be a matter of life or death, namely, the effectiveness of condoms in preventing the transmission of HIV. Any legislation that states develop must, therefore, include language mandating medical accuracy in all curricula.

Laws Should Mandate Education Topics

Unfortunately, it would not be enough to require that all information in sexuality education curricula be medically accurate because that would allow programs simply to remove all references to condoms and other necessary topics, thus conforming with the letter, if not spirit, of the law. So, in addition to a medical accuracy requirement, laws must also ensure that certain topics are covered in any sex education class, such as HIV/AIDS, condoms and contraceptives, STDs, pregnancy, and family planning options. Only when it is law that these topics are covered in a sex education class in a medically accurate way will young people have a fair shot at gaining the information necessary to protect themselves.

Of course, any law should also mandate that sex education classes are taught in the first place, at regular intervals, over a young person's school career. For an example of an extremely well-crafted sex education law, look no further than the state of Oregon. A summary of Oregon's law and other health information can be found at www.siecus.org/oregon2009.

This article has focused primarily on the case for comprehensive sexuality education based on its effectiveness and the need for medical accuracy. These issues, however, are only one piece of the pie. The CDC's Youth Risk Behavior Surveillance Survey, suggested reading for anyone who wants to thoroughly depress him- or herself, reveals that more than 10 percent of young people report that they have *never* been taught about HIV/AIDS. This is inexcusable and remedying this situation should be a national priority. Furthermore, there are many, many disproportionately affected groups such as racial and ethnic minorities, LGBT individuals, and men who have sex with men that are falling further and further behind the national averages in virtually every important sexual health statistic.

The need to support comprehensive sexuality education over abstinence-only-until-marriage programs should not be about political gamesmanship or the culture wars, although, too often, it appears that it is. Instead, the focus should be on providing young people and the most affected members of society with the tools and information they need to protect themselves, their health, and their future.

Periodical and Internet Sources Bibliography

The following articles have been chosen to supplement the diverse views presented in this chapter.

Advocates for Youth	"Comprehensive Sex Education: Research and Results," September 2009. www.advocatesforyouth.org.
Wendy Gittleson	"Planned Parenthood and the Teen Pregnancy 'Epidemic,'" *Social Justice Examiner*, April 12, 2011.
Kierra Johnson	"The Myth of the Teen Pregnancy Epidemic," *Huffington Post*, July 21, 2010. www.huffingtonpost.com.
Christine Kim and Robert Rector	"Executive Summary: Evidence on the Effectiveness of Abstinence Education: An Update," The Heritage Foundation, February 19, 2010.
Kim Krisberg	"Teen Pregnancy Prevention Focusing on Evidence," *Nation's Health*, April 2010.
Olivia Marshall	"The Drop Out Crisis and Teen Pregnancy," June 29, 2011. www.progressivepolicy.org.
National Abstinence Education Association	"Frequently Asked Questions— Correcting Misinformation in the Sex Ed Debate," 2010. www.abstinenceassociation.org.
Robert Rector	"The President's New Sex Ed: So Long, Love, Abstinence, and Marriage," *National Review*, April 5, 2010.
Nancy Rommelmann	"Anatomy of a Child Pornographer: What Happens When Adults Catch Teenagers 'Sexting' Photos to Each Other? The Death of Common Sense," *Reason*, vol. 41, no. 3, July 2009.

How Should Society Deal with Teen Discipline and Teen Crime?

Chapter Preface

The current rate of violent crimes committed by teens is significantly lower than any other time during the past twenty years—well below the peak levels seen in the mid-1990s. However, a very high percentage of teens continue to get arrested and are drawn into the legal system, creating a criminal arrest record that remains for years. A recent study of arrest rates, led by criminologist Robert Brame and published in the December 19, 2011, online edition of *Pediatrics*, concludes, "The criminal justice system has clearly become more aggressive in dealing with offenders since the 1960s." By the age of eighteen, more than 20 percent of teens will have been arrested at least once.

In schools, teens are disciplined and frequently arrested for a wide array of offenses. In a widely publicized incident in May 2012, a Texas teenager and honor student who was working two jobs to help support her family spent a night in jail for missing too many classes. Though not all student offenses lead to arrest, the disciplinary problems of students today are being punished at rates unheard of twenty years ago. According to a 2012 study of the Texas school system by Deborah Fowler, "Six in ten public school students were suspended or expelled at least once between their seventh and twelfth grade school years." The impetus behind this prominent trend is the Texas zero tolerance policy.

Zero tolerance policies have been enforced rigorously in schools in recent years, and much student behavior that was formerly treated as a matter for school discipline is now routinely referred to the legal system. Critics of this shift have called it the "school to prison pipeline." Is the best way to handle teenage offenses through stricter law enforcement and harsher punishments, or are there better ways to handle teen disciplinary problems? Authors debate issues related to teen misbehavior and punishment in the following chapter.

> *"For both liberal and conservative opponents of antigay bullying, it boils down to the issue of basic human dignity."*

Bullying of Gay Teens Is a Serious Problem

Kenneth Miller

The following viewpoint discusses incidents of gay teens who committed suicide after extensive bullying. Because homosexuality is more widely accepted than ever before, the author says, the problem is garnering the attention of both liberals and conservatives who believe that a safe environment is a human right for all teens. Kenneth Miller is an award-winning writer and editor whose work has appeared in many leading US magazines.

As you read, consider the following questions:

1. According to the viewpoint, what percentage of gay, lesbian, and bisexual teens have attempted suicide?
2. The viewpoint makes clear that the most important support system for gay teens to avoid thoughts of suicide is whom?

3. Gay or lesbian kids realize their orientation around what age, according to the viewpoint?

September 9 [2010] Billy Lucas, age 15, of Greensburg, Indiana, hanged himself from the rafters of his family's barn. September 19: Seth Walsh, 13, of Tehachapi, California, hanged himself from a tree in his yard. September 22: Tyler Clementi, 18, a Rutgers University freshman, jumped off the George Washington Bridge in New York City. September 23: Asher Brown, 13, of Houston, Texas, shot himself in the head. These four boys didn't know each other, but they did have something in common. They'd been bullied at school, and one by one, they all apparently came to the same conclusion: If you're gay or thought to be gay, life just isn't worth living.

Homophobia and US Culture

For most Americans the news reports were heartbreaking. They took us beyond our political arguments over gay marriage and "Don't Ask, Don't Tell"—even past our deeper disagreements about homosexuality. For once we could all agree: Those kids should be in their classrooms, not in caskets.

September's gruesome trend raised pressing questions. Homosexuality appears to be more widely tolerated than ever: Fifty-two percent of Americans consider it morally acceptable, according to a recent Gallup poll. Kids can join gay-straight alliance groups at more than 4,000 high schools and more than 150 middle schools nationwide and find advice and support online. Yet according to the *Journal of Adolescent Health*, about one-third of gay, lesbian, and bisexual teens report an attempt at suicide. Why are so many still driven to try to take their own life?

"Despite recent cultural shifts, kids still get the overwhelming message from society that homosexuality is not acceptable," says Scott Quasha, PsyD, a professor of school psychology at Brooklyn College. It's not uncommon to hear fierce condemnation from politicians and preachers as they debate gay civil rights. Homosexuality is compared to incest, bestiality, even violent crime. "This trickles down into the schools, where bullying occurs," says Dr. Quasha. "A gay child is an easy target for classmates looking to make trouble."

The Pressure of Gender Norms

Antigay bullying is something all parents should be concerned about, says Merle Bennett Buzzelli, who oversees the public school antiviolence program in Akron, Ohio. "The victims are not just students who are actually gay," she points out—the abuse is also directed at straight kids who don't quite fit gender norms. Tomboyish girls and guys who show interest in, say, gymnastics or dance are often called the same names—and subjected to the same ostracism and attacks—as their gay and lesbian classmates. There's no evidence that Billy Lucas was gay, but he was "different," classmates said. Because of that, bullies called him "fag" and told him he didn't deserve to live. Of course, for kids who do experience same-sex attraction, the use of the word gay as an all-purpose put-down is just one more painful indication that they don't fit in, whether or not they look or act any different from their peers, says Dr. Quasha.

"Being a teenager is tough enough," says Jody M. Huckaby, executive director of Parents, Families, and Friends of Lesbians and Gays (PFLAG), a national organization. "There's so much peer pressure. And when you're constantly getting messages that you're not okay, the pressure can just be too much. For some kids, it's hard to imagine that life will ever get better."

The Power of Parents

Since parents of gay kids are generally not gay themselves, even the most loving can find it hard to know how to respond when their child comes out. When Rashad Davis was 15, his mom, Deon Davis, sensed that there was something he wasn't telling her. "He was very, very depressed," recalls Deon, 44, a dialysis nurse from Fort Lauderdale, Florida. "I'd say, 'Honey, please talk to me, you know I can handle it.' He'd say, 'No, Mom, it's just school,' and go to his room. Then, driving him to school one day, I saw cuts all over his arm. I asked if he was hurting himself and he said yes."

Afraid that Rashad might be suicidal, Deon called his health-insurance plan, which sent a therapist directly to their home. A few weeks later, with the therapist present, Rashad told his mom the source of his agony: He'd realized he was gay and he was terrified that family and friends would reject him. "I took a big swallow," says Deon. "I forced myself to say 'okay' and hug him, but then I went off and cried all night long."

Deon was confused—this was the last thing she expected. "Rashad was 200 percent boy," she explains. "He wanted to play every sport and do every boy thing." And despite what she'd told her son, she really wasn't okay with it at all. "I'd been taught in my family and church that being gay was wrong and I thought that Rashad was going to go to hell. I thought, 'This is disgusting. What are people going to say about us? My sister, his father, my father. . . .'"

Still, something told her she'd better not share her fears with Rashad, and she was soon grateful to have made that decision. A week later Rashad told her about the antigay bullying he'd been experiencing at school. "I don't care if anybody else accepts me as long as you do," he told her. That comment really changed her attitude. "I knew I would have to be his protector and guide," she says.

Finding Ways to Support Gay Teens

It wasn't easy. To cope with her negative feelings, Deon began working with the therapist, connected with PFLAG, and read up on gay issues. Bolstered by his mom's support, Rashad soon transferred to a more accepting high school. "I regained my confidence and started smiling more," he recalls. Now 19, Rashad is doing well as a sophomore at Florida Gulf Coast University.

Deon Davis played it exactly right, says clinical social worker Caitlin Ryan, PhD, director of the Family Acceptance Project

Gay, Lesbian, and Bisexual Teens

Yet another important aspect of the general sexual environment of kids is the corrosive effect of homophobia on kids with same-sex orientation—the gay and lesbian teenagers who comprise about 10 percent of the adolescent population. One of the best treatments of how gay and lesbian kids experience adolescence is to be found in a book by psychologist Ritch Savin-Williams titled *Mom, Dad, I'm Gay: How Families Negotiate Coming Out. . . .* In our own research with college students, we found that 10 percent of the male students said they had same-sex orientations during high school, but only 63 percent of these males said their parents were aware of it at the time.

In our study of the secret life of teenagers, we found that 10 percent of the female students reported they had a lesbian orientation in high school, and that 90 percent of their parents never knew. The bottom line in all this is that parents should not assume that homophobia at school is "somebody else's problem." If for no other reason than that our own beloved children may be targeted, we should all be concerned that emotionally vulnerable kids are being tormented through this special form of sexual harassment that is rampant in our society and in our schools.

James Garbarino and Ellen de Lara,
And Words Can Hurt Forever. *New York:*
The Free Press, 2002, p. 91.

at San Francisco State University. After almost a decade of research on gay, lesbian, bisexual, and transgender teens, Dr. Ryan's group has found a clear pattern: The more supportive the parents and family, the better kids do over the long run. "That doesn't necessarily mean changing your deeply held beliefs," Dr. Ryan explains. "It means finding a way to balance those beliefs with the love you have for your child."

Many parents, unwilling to believe that their child is gay, try to talk him out of it; they may tell him he's going through a phase, forbid him to discuss it, and keep him from reaching out to the gay community. Often, their motive is to protect their child from harassment. But this well-meaning approach tends to backfire, Dr. Ryan says, since the child interprets it as a rejection of his true self: If his parents won't accept him for what he is, who will?

As young adults, gay kids from highly rejecting families are more than eight times as likely to attempt suicide, almost six times as likely to be clinically depressed, and more than three times as likely to abuse drugs or be at high risk for HIV infection than those from families who are more accepting, Dr. Ryan's research has found. But even small changes can yield big results, she says—children from families that are only moderately rejecting have significantly fewer problems.

Even parents who can't be fully accepting can find ways to be supportive. "You can say, 'I think this is wrong but I love you and I'm going to be here for you,'" Dr. Ryan suggests. "Be willing to listen. Give your child a hug."

Tolerance Can Save Lives

Even if their parents fully support them, some gay kids are overwhelmed by community intolerance. Soon after Tyler Clementi's fatal leap, openly gay 19-year-old Zach Harrington killed himself in his hometown of Norman, Oklahoma. He had recently attended a city council meeting in which homosexuality was called a "destructive lifestyle" that corrupts children. Zach's parents felt that the rancorous debate may have pushed their son over the edge, the town's newspaper reported.

We all need to speak more carefully, says Father Mike Tegeder, pastor of the Church of St. Edward in Bloomington, Minnesota. "The Catholic Church teaches that each person has dignity, whatever their race or gender or sexual orientation," he says. "We don't need to agree with one another, but we have to respect one another's dignity as children of God."

And many religious groups agree. Exodus International, a conservative Christian organization that had previously encouraged kids to speak out against homosexuality, changed direction after the recent string of suicides, deciding to advocate "biblical tolerance and grace" instead of confrontation. For Warren Throckmorton, PhD, an associate professor of psychology at Grove City College, a Christian school in Pennsylvania, the group's reversal was an obvious choice. "It seems to me that Christians should be first in line in saying that everyone should be treated the way you yourself want to be treated," says Dr. Throckmorton, a traditional evangelical who recently developed The Golden Rule Pledge, a program specifically designed to help conservative churches prevent antigay bullying.

What Communities Can Do

To combat antigay bullying in schools, parents of straight kids need to take a stand, says Maureen Costello, director of Teaching Tolerance, an educational project of the Southern Poverty Law Center, a civil rights organization. "We have to tell our children that bullying of any kind is unacceptable but we also have to model the behavior we expect of them." Expressing your opinions in a civil way, whether on homosexuality or any other issue, is a good place to start, Costello suggests.

Concerned citizens can also push for schools to adopt antibullying policies that specifically cover harassment because of sexual or gender identity, Costello says. Many people feel a blanket "respect for all" statement is enough, but research shows such policies aren't as effective at protecting students from antigay bullying.

Teachers might let it ride if a kid says "that's so gay," since the insult isn't always intended as an antihomosexual slur, Buzzelli explains. Yet it still creates a hostile environment for gay kids.

So her bullying prevention program starts by explaining to kids that the term refers to an entire group of people. "Using gay as a put-down is like using Jew or black or disabled as a put-down—it's not acceptable," Buzzelli says. "Middle school kids also throw around words like fag and dyke without thinking about what they mean," she adds. They need to know these words are as offensive to gays as racial slurs are to people of color.

How to Create a Safe Environment for Gay Students

Buzzelli's team focuses its bullying-prevention efforts on middle schools since that's when kids become aware of their sexuality, and it's also when bullying is often at its worst. When Seth Walsh killed himself at 13, many Americans were surprised by his youth: How could he even have known his sexual orientation at that age? That wasn't unusual, experts say: Research shows that kids first become aware of sexual feelings around 10 and those who are gay or lesbian know it around 13, just the way straight kids know they are attracted to the opposite sex.

If parents balk at terms like gay being discussed in middle school, Buzzelli explains to them that efforts to prevent bullying are crucial to their own child's ability to get an education. If bullying goes on, it creates a chaotic environment where no one can learn.

Cara Riggs is principal at Omaha South High Magnet School, another school that insists on a safe environment for gay students. Riggs has little patience for those who feel the school is advancing some kind of radical agenda: "We're not advocating anything but respect," she tells them. Dr. Throckmorton concurs: "Mutual respect and freedom from hostility are Christian virtues," he says. And as the Department of Education reminded schools in an October 26 [2010] letter, harassment of any kind is against federal civil rights law.

For both liberal and conservative opponents of antigay bullying, it boils down to the issue of basic human dignity. "As a parent, it's your responsibility to sit your kids down and explain how there are lots of different kinds of people," says Dr. Quasha. "You can even say, 'In our religion, we don't really agree with this, but what we do believe is that everybody deserves to be treated with kindness and respect.'"

"It's one thing to hold bullies responsible for their own actions, but it's trickier to blame them for the chain of events that may follow."

Teenage Bullying Should Not Be Treated as a Crime

Jessica Bennett

In the following viewpoint, Jessica Bennett concedes that anti-gay bullying has contributed significantly to a rise in gay suicides in recent years. But she argues that bullying, in most cases, is just one factor among many in the decision to commit suicide. The young people involved in some of the more prominent cases of bullying and gay suicide were too immature to see the ramifications of their behavior and don't deserve to go to jail, according to Bennett. Bennett is a senior writer and editor at both Newsweek *and the* Daily Beast; *she covers social issues, gender, sex, and culture.*

As you read, consider the following questions:

1. According to the viewpoint, what is the main difference between bullying a half century ago and bullying today?

Jessica Bennett, "From Lockers to Lockup," Newsweek, vol. 156, no. 15, October 11, 2010. Copyright © 2010 by Newsweek, Inc. All rights reserved. Reprinted by permission.

2. What was one of the felony charges noted in the viewpoint that was brought against the bullies in the Phoebe Prince case?

3. What punishment did the six students in the Phoebe Prince case ultimately receive, according to the viewpoint?

School bullying in the digital age can have tragic consequences. But should it be a crime?

It started with rumors, a love triangle, and a dirty look in a high-school bathroom. Soon jokes about an "Irish slut" cropped up on Facebook, and a girl's face was scribbled out of a class photo hanging up at school. One day, in the cafeteria, another girl marched in, pointed at her, and shouted "stay away from other people's men." A week later, as the girl walked home, a car full of students crept close. One kid hurled a crumpled soda can out the window, followed closely by shrieks of "whore!" If your children had behaved like this, how would you want them punished? Certainly a proper grounding would be in order; computer privileges revoked. Detention, yes—maybe even suspension. Or what about 10 years in jail? Now what if we told you that the girl had gone home after the soda-can incident and killed herself—discovered by her little sister, hanging in a stairwell. Now which punishment fits the crime?

The Idea of Being Bullied to Death

This is the conundrum of Phoebe Prince, the 15-year-old South Hadley, Mass., girl the media have already determined was "bullied to death." It's the crime of the moment, the blanket explanation slapped on cases from Texas to California, where two 13-year-old boys recently killed themselves after being tormented for being gay. One of the most shocking examples yet came last week [September 22, 2010], when Tyler Clementi, an 18-year-old New Jersey college student, threw himself off the George Washington Bridge after his roommate and a friend allegedly streamed a Webcam video of his tryst with a man. Cases like these are being invoked as potent symbols for why, in the digital age, schools need strong bullying policies and states need stronger legislation.

But do they? Is the notion of being bullied to death valid? It's one thing to hold bullies responsible for their own actions, but it's trickier to blame them for the chain of events that may follow. No one would deny that Clementi's roommate did the unconscionable—the alleged crime is all the more disturbing because of the specter of antigay bias. Yet they couldn't have known how badly the stunt would end. Now he and his friend face up to five years in prison for invasion of privacy. In the case of Phoebe Prince, the answer of who's to blame might change if you knew that she had tried to kill herself before the epithets, was on medication for depression, and was struggling with her parents' separation. So where is the line now between behavior that's bad and behavior that's criminal? Does the definition of old-school bullying need to be rewritten for the new-media age?

The Rise of Anti-Bullying Laws

In effect, it already has been. Forty-five states now have anti-bullying laws; in Massachusetts, which has one of the strictest, anti-bullying programs are mandated in schools, and criminal punishment is outlined in the text for even the youngest offenders. It's a good-will effort, to be sure—prevention programs have been shown to reduce school bullying by as much as 50 percent. With 1 in 5 students bullied each year—and an appalling 9 in 10 gay and lesbian students—that's good news: kids who are bullied are five times more likely to be depressed, and nearly 160,000 of them skip school each day, fearful of their peers. Bullies themselves don't fare well, either: one study, of middle-school boys, found that 60 percent of those deemed "bullies" would be convicted of at least one crime by the time they reached 24.

But forget, for the moment, the dozens of articles that have called bullying a "pandemic"—because the opposite is true.

School bullying can be devastating, but social scientists say it is no more extreme, nor more prevalent, than it was a half century ago. In fact, says Dan Olweus, a leading bullying expert, new data shows rates of school bullying may have even gone down over the past decade. Today's world of cyberbullying is different, yes—far-reaching, more visually potent, and harder to wash away than comments scrawled on a bathroom wall. All of which can make it harder to combat. But it still happens a third less than traditional bullying, says Olweus.

The reality may be that while the incidence of bullying has remained relatively the same, it's our reaction to it that's changed: the helicopter parents who want to protect their kids from every stick and stone, the cable-news commentators who whip them into a frenzy, the insta-vigilantism of the Internet. When it comes down to it, bullying is not just a social ill; it's a "cottage industry," says Suffolk Law School's David Yamada—complete with commentators and prevention experts and a new breed of legal scholars, all preparing to take on an enemy that's always been there. None of this is to say that bullying is not a serious problem, or that tackling it is not important. But like a stereo with the volume turned too high, all the noise distorts the facts, making it nearly impossible to judge when a case is somehow criminal, or merely cruel.

Understanding the Crime

To make sense of the punishment, of course, we must first understand the crime. Phoebe Prince's problems at South Hadley High School began around November of last year [2009], when the freshman became involved with two senior boys—Austin Renaud and Sean Mulveyhill, the school's star football player—both of whom had girlfriends. According to their indictments, the boys, their girlfriends, and students Ashley Longe and Sharon Velasquez engaged in what the DA [district attorney] described as a "nearly three-month campaign" of verbal assault and physical threats against Phoebe. What appears to be the worst of the

When Bullying Results in Suicide

[The Tyler Clementi and Phoebe Prince] suicide cases raise the broad question of whether adolescents who engage in bullying and cyberbullying should be open to criminal charges when the outcome is tragic. Facts and circumstances of the cases matter, of course, but experts say issues of psychology, legal philosophy and science—specifically dealing with adolescent brain development and maturity—also have a role. . . .

Nonetheless, [Professor Justin W.] Patchin says the "hue and cry" to criminalize cyberbullying is "misguided." Following Clementi's death, Patchin wrote that "the vast majority of cyberbullying incidents can and should be handled informally: with parents, schools and others working together to address the problem before it rises to the level of a violation of criminal law."

If bullying results in a suicide, he says in an interview, "probably somebody should be held to a higher sanction." But, he adds, "we already have existing statutes that would do. We certainly shouldn't pass a new law saying that if you cyberbully somebody and they commit suicide, you're going to get life without parole. That would be a mistake."

Thomas J. Billitteri, "Preventing Bullying,"
CQ Researcher, *vol. 20, no. 43, December 10,*
2010, pp. 12–13. http://library.cqpress.com
/cqresearcher.

crimes involves a threat to "beat Phoebe up"; repeated taunts of "whore" and "Irish slut"; and, on the day of her death, the soda-can incident, which left Phoebe in tears. When Phoebe got home that afternoon, she texted a friend: "I can't do it anymore." Her sister found her body at 4:30 P.M.

Her death, understandably, sent South Hadley into a shame-and-blame spiral. The school principal opened an internal investigation, but allowed the then-unidentified bullies to remain in class. A community member sympathetic to Phoebe's story went to the *Boston Globe*, which published a column chastising school officials for allowing the "mean girls" to remain in school, "defiant, unscathed." A Facebook group with the headline "Expel the three girls who caused Phoebe Prince to commit suicide" suddenly had thousands of fans. School officials took to the press—defending how they could have let the bullying go on, asserting they had only learned of the problem the week before Phoebe's death. "I'm not naive [enough] to think we'll have zero bullying, but this was a complex tragedy," South Hadley principal Dan Smith tells *Newsweek*.

Felony Charges for Bullying

Enter District Attorney Elizabeth Scheibel, whose profile on the National District Attorneys Association Web site, until recently, detailed how, as a child, she beat up a schoolyard bully who was picking on her brother. On March 29, Scheibel released the names of six students she would indict on felony charges, whose "relentless activity," she said, was "designed to humiliate [Phoebe] and make it impossible for her to remain at school." Since there is no law explicitly making bullying a crime, Scheibel charged two of them with stalking, two with criminal harassment, and five with civil-rights violations resulting in bodily injury, alleging that Phoebe's ability to get an education had been made impossible. She also charged both of the boys with statutory rape, for allegedly having sex with Phoebe while she was underage—an offense punishable by up to three years in jail. The civil-rights violation carries a maximum of 10 years. (All six defendants have pleaded not guilty.)

The law (and the media) may assess the world in black or white, but the players in the case don't fit into neat categories. Phoebe suffered a terrible tragedy, but court filings have since revealed she had her own demons, too. She struggled with depression, self-mutilation, had been prescribed Seroquel (a medication to treat mood disorders), and had attempted suicide once before. By the same token, each of the students charged with bullying Phoebe were in good academic standing, South Hadley's superintendent, Gus Sayer, told *Newsweek*. Does that in any way excuse their behavior? Not at all—and each has been out of school since March, suspended, indefinitely, until their case is resolved in court. . . . But do they deserve to go to jail? "These are not the troubled kids we sometimes deal with," says Sayer. "These are nice kids, regular kids. They come from nice families. They were headed to college. And now, in addition to losing Phoebe, we're losing [them] too." (Phoebe's father, Jeremy Prince, has said he would ask the court for leniency if the teens confessed and apologized.)

Lives Are Forever Changed

Still, even if they are acquitted, it's clear the lives of the accused are forever altered. None completed school last year; Mulveyhill has already lost a football scholarship. Angeles Chanon, the mother of Sharon Velasquez, says her daughter is studying for her GED, but heartbroken that she can't return to class this fall. Since there aren't any other public high schools in South Hadley—and public schools in Massachusetts can deny entrance based on a felony charge—her options for continuing on a different campus are slim, and her mother, also a full-time student, can't afford a private school. In the meantime, Sharon is still haunted by the tragedy of Phoebe's death. She sits at home most days, reading, watching TV—but scared to leave the house alone. Sharon's family has received death threats, prank calls, and a rock thrown through a second-story window, along with a stream of nasty unsigned letters delivered to her door. Some call for her to be "raped and killed"; others hurl insults and racial slurs. "I don't know if I can even describe what my family has been through," says Chanon, who agreed to speak to *Newsweek* with her lawyer,

Colin Keefe, present. "The cameras in our faces, the harassment, the letters—I'd come home and people would be in the parking lot waiting for me."

The irony, of course, is that it all sounds a bit like the kind of torment Phoebe allegedly endured. But if these kids are bullies according to the law, what about the people around them? Massachusetts's anti-bullying statute defines bullying as repeated behavior that, among other things, "causes emotional harm" or "creates a hostile environment" at school. If it were applied to the real world, wouldn't most of us be bullies? It's easy to see how the blossoming field of bullying law could ultimately criminalize the kind of behavior we engage in every day—not just in schoolyards, but in workplaces, in politics, at home. "You're not going to prevent a lot of this stuff," says former New York prosecutor Sam Goldberg, a Boston criminal attorney. "It may seem harsh, but to some degree, you're going to have to tell your kid, 'Sometimes people say mean things.'"

Kids Deserve a Second Chance

What most bullying experts and legal scholars agree on is that prosecution—in the Prince case, anyway—may be the worst possible scenario. There is longstanding research to show that law is not a deterrent to kids who respond emotionally to their surroundings; ultimately, labeling a group of raucous teens as "criminals" will only make it harder for them to engage with society when they return. Certainly, there is behavior that should be treated as a crime—the story of Clementi, the young Rutgers student who jumped off the bridge, is particularly hard to stomach. But many kids "just mess up," says Sameer Hinduja, a criminologist at Florida Atlantic University, and the codirector of the Cyberbullying Research Center. "They react emotionally, and most of them express a lot of remorse. I think most kids deserve another chance." [In 2011, all the accused students in the Prince case were sentenced to community service and probation, or to probation only.]

> *"We now have overwhelming evidence showing that wholesale incarceration of juvenile offenders is a counterproductive public policy."*

Juvenile Detention Is an Ineffective Teen Sentencing Policy

Richard A. Mendel/The Annie E. Casey Foundation

Richard A. Mendel argues in the following viewpoint that the current juvenile justice system, which relies heavily on mass incarceration of teen offenders, is badly broken. The violence and abuse within youth facilities is bad enough, according to Mendel, but these institutions also fail to rehabilitate the youth within them. Mendel is an independent writer and researcher specializing in poverty-related issues in youth, youth crime prevention, and juvenile justice. He has written five major publications for the Annie E. Casey Foundation, a private charitable organization dedicated to the welfare of disadvantaged children.

As you read, consider the following questions:

1. According to the author, the United States incarcerates

youth offenders at a rate how much higher than the next nation in the world?

2. Do juvenile correction facilities reduce criminal activity for those youth who pass through them, according to the viewpoint?

3. As cited by the viewpoint, what is one reason that juvenile correction populations have decreased?

For more than a century, the predominant strategy for the treatment and punishment of serious and sometimes not-so-serious juvenile offenders in the United States has been placement into large juvenile corrections institutions, alternatively known as training schools, reformatories, or youth corrections centers.

The United States Relies on Juvenile Incarceration

Excluding the roughly 25,000 youth held in detention centers daily awaiting their court trials or pending placement to a correctional program, the latest official national count of youth in correctional custody, conducted in 2007, found that roughly 60,500 U.S. youth were confined in correctional facilities or other residential programs each night on the order of a juvenile delinquency court. For perspective, that's more adolescents than currently reside in mid-sized American cities like Louisville, Kentucky; Nashville, Tennessee; Baltimore, Maryland; or Portland, Oregon. A high proportion of these confined youth are minorities. According to the most recent national count, two of every five confined youth are African Americans and one-fifth are Hispanic; non-Hispanic white youth, who comprise three-fifths of the total youth population, were just 37 percent of the confined youth.

America's heavy reliance on juvenile incarceration is unique among the world's developed nations. Though juvenile violent crime arrest rates are only marginally higher in the United States than in many other nations, a recently published international comparison found that America's youth custody rate (including youth in both detention and correctional custody) was 336 of every 100,000 youth in 2002—nearly five times the rate of the next highest nation (69 per 100,000 in South Africa). A number of nations essentially don't incarcerate minors at all. In other words, mass incarceration of troubled and troublemaking adolescents is neither inevitable nor necessary in a modern society.

State juvenile corrections systems in the United States confine youth in many types of facilities, including group homes, residential treatment centers, boot camps, wilderness programs, or county-run youth facilities (some of them locked, others secured only through staff supervision). But the largest share of committed youth—about 40 percent of the total—are held in locked long-term youth correctional facilities operated primarily by state governments or by private firms under contract to states. These facilities are usually large, with many holding 200–300 youth. They typically operate in a regimented (prison-like) fashion, and feature correctional hardware such as razor-wire, isolation cells, and locked cell blocks.

Juvenile Incarceration Does Not Reduce Crime

Yet these institutions have never been found to reduce the criminality of troubled young people. Quite the opposite: For decades now, follow-up studies tracking youth released from juvenile corrections facilities have routinely reported high rates of recidivism. Meanwhile, reports of pervasive violence and abuse have been regularly emerging from these facilities for as long as anyone can remember.

Nonetheless, incarceration in secure congregate-care youth corrections facilities has persisted as the signature characteristic and the biggest budget line item of most state juvenile justice systems across the nation. This status quo has been buttressed in part by public fears of youth crime and by politicians' fears of being labeled "soft" on crime. The aversion to change has been further reinforced by the closely guarded economic interests of communities that host these facilities—and of the workers employed to staff them. Finally, states' continuing reliance on these institutions has been abetted by a lack of proven alternatives: if not correctional confinement for youthful offenders, what? Until the 1980s, juvenile crime prevention and treatment experts had few answers.

However, an avalanche of research has emerged over the past three decades about what works and doesn't work in combating juvenile crime. This report provides a detailed review of this research, and it comes to the following conclusion: We now have overwhelming evidence showing that wholesale incarceration of juvenile offenders is a counterproductive public policy. While a small number of youthful offenders pose a serious threat to the public and must be confined, incarcerating a broader swath of the juvenile offender population provides no benefit for public safety. It wastes vast sums of taxpayer dollars. And more often than not, it harms the well-being and dampens the future prospects of the troubled and lawbreaking youth who get locked up. Other approaches usually produce equal or better results— sometimes far better—at a fraction of the cost.

Views on Juvenile Incarceration Are Changing

The idea of shuttering youth corrections facilities and substantially shrinking the number of youth in confinement may sound radical. But the reality is that in large swaths of the nation—on the east coast, west coast, and in middle America, in big states and small, red states and blue—it's already happening. Often prompted by lawsuits and revelations of abuse, or by mounting budget pressures, or by studies showing high recidivism, many states have slashed their juvenile corrections populations in recent years—causing no observable increase in juvenile crime

Training Delinquents

When peer-based treatment programs for delinquent teens were first created, the idea behind them was considered novel and appealing: Peers are an incredibly powerful force in adolescence, so why not make delinquency-prevention programs peer-focused? Kids would rather sit with groups of other teens than be lectured by an adult any day. The idea had such appeal that programs sprang up all over the country. Some were residential—dealing with teens already incarcerated, or at least assigned to live outside the home, based on their behavior. Others were run in schools. Some targeted highly delinquent kids; others targeted those who simply showed early risk factors for future delinquency. All of the programs began with high hopes.

Over and over again, however, evaluations of these programs kept arriving at the same unsettling results. These programs consistently had small effects in the direction of making delinquent behavior *worse* among the youths who participated in them. It was [psychologist] Tom [Dishion] who figured out why. He pieced together what was happening by conducting two carefully controlled studies in which he showed that the solution was in fact the problem: Putting together groups of at-risk youths consistently tended to increase their likelihood of becoming delinquent over time because teens formed their own miniculture, and it wasn't a miniculture adults would feel good about. As long as the peers were left mainly to interact with one another, there was little the adults in these programs could do to change this culture.

Joseph Allen and Claudia Worrell Allen,
Escaping the Endless Adolescence. *New York:*
Ballantine Books, 2009, pp. 67–68.

rates. The trend is continuing, though the pace of change remains uneven—in part because the isolated changes are occurring largely under the radar, not as part of any organized movement. The winds of change are blowing, but they have not yet gathered gale-force intensity.

The evidence is clear that these changes must continue. The weight of expert opinion solidly concurs.

"We have to recognize that incarceration of youth per se is toxic," says Dr. Barry Krisberg, the longtime president of the National Council on Crime and Delinquency now on faculty at the University of California-Berkeley, "so we need to reduce incarceration of young people to the very small dangerous few. And we've got to recognize that if we lock up a lot of kids, it's going to increase crime."

Douglas Abrams, a juvenile justice scholar at the University of Missouri, concluded in 2007 that "More than a century after the creation of the nation's first juvenile court grounded in rehabilitative impulses, many states still maintain inhumane, thoroughly ineffective juvenile prisons that neither rehabilitate children nor protect public safety."

The Juvenile Corrections System Is Counterproductive

"The best word to describe America's addiction to training schools is 'iatrogenic'—a cure that makes problems worse," says Paul DeMuro, who served as commissioner of the Pennsylvania juvenile corrections system in the late 1970s and has since served as an expert witness in numerous legal cases concerning conditions of confinement in juvenile facilities. "The model has been around for 150 years, and has proven a failure by any measure."

The main body of this report details six pervasive flaws in the states' long-standing heavy reliance on large, prison-like correctional institutions. Specifically, the report will show that these facilities are frequently: (1) dangerous, (2) ineffective, (3) unnecessary, (4) obsolete, (5) wasteful, and (6) inadequate. A subsequent chapter addresses the question of public safety, finding that states where juvenile confinement was sharply reduced in recent years experienced more favorable trends in juvenile crime than jurisdictions which maintained or increased their correctional facility populations. . . .

The time has come for states to embrace a fundamentally different orientation to treating adolescent offenders—an approach grounded in evidence that promises to be far more humane, cost-effective, and protective of public safety than our time-worn and counterproductive reliance on juvenile incarceration.

> *"The zero tolerance phrase has taken on a life of its own and . . . been exaggerated for the purpose of either supporting or opposing other school safety strategies."*

Problems with Zero Tolerance Policies Have Been Exaggerated

Ken Trump

In the following viewpoint, Ken Trump argues that school security systems have been unfairly targeted as part of the criticism of zero tolerance policies. He contends that school security involves much more than metal detectors, surveillance cameras, and security officers. It also involves training, crisis preparedness planning, and other important elements. Trump is a school security consultant and president of National School Safety and Security Services.

As you read, consider the following questions:

1. How does the author describe the typical discipline policy of most school administrators?

2. According to the viewpoint, why aren't metal detectors, cameras, and security officers enough to make a school secure?

3. Who does Trump repeatedly blame for the unfair rap on school security?

"Zero tolerance" has been a political buzzword for so many years now that it has more meaning in the minds of academicians and politicians than it does in day-to-day practice by school administrators.

Zero Tolerance Is Not to Blame

In well over 25 years of school safety experience with school officials in 50 states, we have consistently found the vast majority of school administrators to strive for firm, fair, and consistent discipline applied with good common sense. Unfortunately, there are anecdotal incidents from time to time which lack the latter part of the equation: The common sense.

It is these cases that get labeled as "zero tolerance" by critics who falsely try to create a perception that there is some type of mass conspiracy by educators to unfairly discipline children. Contrary to suggestions by the media, politicians, and Ivory-Tower [academic] theorists, the real problem is therefore the absence of common sense and questionable implementation of disciplinary policies, not the presence of intentionally harsh actions committed to fuel a master nationwide conspiracy plan called "zero tolerance."

Schools have also developed tunnel vision focus in training school administrators on how to improve test scores, but often fail to provide adequate training on discipline and school safety issues. Proper training of school administrators on school board policies, disciplinary procedures, and overall school safety issues can reduce the risks of questionable actions by school administrators.

School Administrators Are Too Lenient

If anything, our experience has shown that just the opposite exists: Many educators tend to bend over backwards to give students more breaks than they will ever receive out on the streets of our society and in the workplace where we are supposed to be preparing them to function. We can count many, many more instances where we have seen far too lax discipline in our schools than we can count cases where the discipline administered was overly harsh and abusively punitive as some critics want to suggest.

In the end, those kids who receive less than firm, fair, and consistent discipline end up being taught that there are no consequences for inappropriate—and sometimes illegal—behavior as long as it occurs within the grounds of those schools having administrators who are often more worried about keeping their disciplinary and criminal incident reports down for the sake of their own career advancement.

To keep it in perspective, the VAST MAJORITY of school administrators strive for that target of firm, fair, and consistent discipline. The average school administrator is not an extremist on either end of the continuum.

Perhaps most alarming is how the zero tolerance phrase has taken on a life of its own and how it has been exaggerated for the purpose of either supporting or opposing other school safety strategies. For example, academic and "think tank" reports use zero tolerance as a backdrop to promote prevention programs while discrediting school security practices.

The Complexity of School Security Programs

These reports typically err, however, by inaccurately and narrowly defining school security to mean metal detectors, surveillance cameras, school security personnel, School Resource Officers (SROs) or other police in schools, locker searches, and/

or school uniforms. Most school security specialists agree that professional school security programs are much more comprehensive and include security policies and procedures, crime prevention training, crisis preparedness planning, physical design evaluation, coordination with public safety officials, and numerous other components. While these other tools and strategies may be a necessary and appropriate part of many school safety plans, truly professional school security programs are much more encompassing than one or two single approaches.

It is also particularly interesting that the primary basis for many of these reports' anti-security and anti-police arguments rest upon the absence of formal academic studies of school security and school policing programs. Ironically, these reports typically fail to also point out that a number of academic evaluations have identified major weaknesses in many prevention and intervention programs, too, and in some cases have indicated that a number of those programs evaluated are simply ineffective. Yet the authors of these reports condemn school security programs (under the guise of zero tolerance) while continuing to promote prevention programs simply because there have indeed been formal evaluations of prevention programs—regardless of the mixed evaluation findings.

How to Create Successful School Safety Plans

Practical experience repeatedly demonstrates that school safety plans need to reflect a balance of strategies focused on prevention, intervention, school climate, firm and fair discipline, mental health support, proactive security measures, crisis preparedness planning, and community networking. Reasonable security and discipline measures must be a part of these plans so that educators can maintain a secure environment in the here-and-now in order for education and prevention programs to have their longer-term impact in the future. Furthermore, professionally utilized SRO and security personnel, security technology, and related measures can and do, in many cases, reduce risks and prevent school violence.

Zero tolerance has taken on a life of its own, but primarily by politicians, academicians, and in some cases the media. We owe it to our students, school staff, and parents to get beyond the political and academic rhetoric of the zero tolerance debate. Improve training for school administrators on board discipline policies, implement student code of conducts fairly and consistently with common sense, and improve school safety in a balanced and rational manner. Deal with each individual case of questionable discipline, but move on to the real work of implementing meaningful, balanced school safety programs such as those enacted by the majority of educators across the nation.

> *"Policing and punitive disciplinary approaches to school safety contribute to a school climate that is actually more dangerous, not safer."*

Zero Tolerance Is a Harmful School Policy for Teens

Annette Fuentes

In the following viewpoint, Annette Fuentes assesses the widespread failure of zero tolerance policies, especially in California and Texas where rates of suspension for minor infractions have skyrocketed. Fuentes contends that sending students into the legal system for minor offenses does not enhance school safety and is counterproductive to the education and well-being of those involved. Fuentes is the author of Lockdown High: When the Schoolhouse Becomes a Jailhouse.

As you read, consider the following questions:
1. According to the viewpoint, the rate of school suspensions is highest in which states?
2. What percentage of school suspensions were for possessing guns or drugs on campus, according to the author?

3. According to the viewpoint, why do critics of zero tolerance claim the policy is discriminatory?

The term "zero tolerance" was first coined during the [Ronald] Reagan presidency and the war on drugs in the 1980s. Congress enacted the Drug-Free Schools and Communities Act in 1986, bringing the war on drugs to school with rules that mandated zero tolerance for any drugs or alcohol on public school grounds. During the [Bill] Clinton administration, Congress took zero tolerance steps further, passing the 1994 Safe and Gun-Free Schools Act, which mandated a one-year expulsion for students who brought a firearm to school and pumped federal departments of Education and Justice funding into antiviolence programs. Youth, especially African American and Latino males, were considered by criminologists like James Q. Wilson and John Dilulio as superpredators who would fuel an explosive juvenile crime wave in coming decades. A half-dozen high-profile school shootings in the early 1990s, punctuated by the 1999 Columbine shootings, cemented the idea that young people and the public schools they inhabited were dangerous places indeed.

The Expansion of Zero Tolerance

Fear of school violence grew and has persisted despite the clear downward trend in documented incidents of violent crime in schools. Since 1993, according to reports issued annually by the National Center for Education Statistics, incidents of violence in school have been steadily dropping. It is a downward trend that echoes the same crime drop in the nation as a whole. But fear of crime in schools has trumped reality and common sense in shaping policies at the state and local school board levels. Zero tolerance, once focused on drugs, alcohol, and guns, now targets an ever-expanding range of behaviors.

In districts across the country, the presence of police inside public schools has led to rising rates of arrests of students for minor violations of disciplinary codes or simple youthful hijinks that in another era would have landed a student in the principal's office. The idea of the "teachable moment," turning a student error into a learning opportunity, is less likely in a schoolhouse where handcuff-wielding cops teach the lesson.

"Things a police officer might not arrest someone in a bar fight for, you're seeing them make arrests in schools for. There are a lot of children arrested for disorderly conduct, which has a very subjective definition. Whoever is standing there gets to define it. It could be a student who refuses to sit down in class, or a spitball," said Judith Browne-Dianis, co-director of the Advancement Project, a civil rights advocacy and policy group.

Students' clothing choices and idle doodling have been viewed through the zero tolerance lens as proof of gang membership, meriting suspension. Examples abound of even young children punished for transgressions. A 2005 Yale Child Study Center study found that pre-kindergarten students were being expelled from school at a rate three times that of K-12 students. In the post-Sept. 11 United States, a collective fear of terrorists has also colored disciplinary policies, as school districts around the country have added to codes of conduct rules that prohibit "terroristic threats."

Suspensions Are Skyrocketing

The most immediate and visible consequence of punitive discipline policies are the skyrocketing numbers of suspensions logged by state school agencies over the last decade. California, with its 6.1 million public school students, recorded 757,000 suspensions of students during the 2009–10 academic year. It was second only to Texas, where 1.6 million suspensions were ordered that same year—and the Lone Star's public school population is just 4.7 million.

According to Breaking Schools' Rules, a groundbreaking 2011 study of Texas' public school disciplinary practices, 54 percent of students in the state were suspended or expelled at least once between 7th and 12th grades. Just 3 percent of all disciplinary actions were for conduct—such as possessing a gun or drugs on campus—that trigger mandatory expulsion or suspension. The other 97 percent were made at the discretion of school administrators for violations of codes of conduct. Black and special education students were most likely to be suspended or expelled. And students suspended or expelled for discretionary violations were three times as likely to have a subsequent brush with the juvenile justice system.

The discriminatory aspects of zero tolerance policies are widespread and well documented. Zero tolerance suspensions are dished out to African American and Latina/o students way out of proportion to their numbers, a disparity Indiana University professor of educational psychology Russell Skiba found goes back 25 years. Skiba and other education researchers suggest that when teachers are inexperienced or come from racial and class backgrounds very different from the students they teach, "cultural discontinuities" can create adversarial dynamics in the classroom. Alienating curriculum, poor classroom management skills, and negative stereotypes of black youth can lead to authoritarian disciplining and overreliance on suspensions. . . .

In the last 20 years, a growing body of literature by academics and mounting caseloads for legal advocates for youth have been documenting the significant harm and ineffectiveness of zero tolerance disciplinary policies for children and youth—especially African Americans and Latina/os. In 2006, the American Psychological Association was impelled by the weight of evidence to take a public stand against zero tolerance. An APA report called punitive discipline harmful to adolescent development and rebutted the idea that school violence is "out of control" and necessitated a zero tolerance approach. In the years since, such evidence has only increased. . . .

The Presence of Police in Schools

Zero tolerance policies have been matched by a police presence in schools that would have been unimaginable a generation ago.

"There's a zero tolerance policy for bringing weapons to school. Do you want to explain how this rolled up newspaper got into your locker?"

"There's a zero tolerance policy for bringing weapons to school. Do you want to explain how the rolled up newspaper got into your locker?," cartoon by Marty Bucela. www .CartoonStock.com.

For example, in Texas, Augustina Reyes, a professor of education at the University of Houston, began researching suspensions in public schools in 1998. Recently, she said, "zero tolerance has escalated to a new level," as police issue tickets for minor student code violations. Disrupting class, using profanity, acting up on a school bus, truancy, and fighting in a school hallway can lead to a class C misdemeanor ticket and a court appearance for the student and her/his parent, plus court costs of up to $500. In the 2007–08 school year, an estimated 275,000 non-traffic class C tickets were issued to juveniles in Texas, she reports. . . .

The Advancement Project investigated policing in several school districts where arrest rates had soared. In 2003 they published *Derailed! The Schoolhouse to Jailhouse Track*. Browne-Dianis, who authored the report, said: "I got into this because I was working with a Mississippi district where the school policy was that any student involved in a fight—even kids in arguments—had to be sent to youth court, where they could get fined $15 to $500 or probation of six months to a year. I never suspected when I [started looking] at this data that we would be finding children arrested for disorderly conduct or battery on a school board employee."

Policing and punitive disciplinary approaches to school safety contribute to a school climate that is actually more dangerous, not safer. Education professors Matthew Mayer and Peter Leone studied school violence and strategies for creating safer schools back in 1999 and found that schools with more security measures—including metal detectors, locked doors, and security guards—paradoxically had a "higher level of disorder." They called it a "cycle of disorder" in which such restrictions and controls actually created a "reciprocal, destructive relationship" with students . . . who live in a "heightened state of fear." . . .

Alternatives to Zero Tolerance Exist

Palm Beach, Fla., was one of the districts featured in the *Derailed!* study. The district's police department was arresting students at astronomical rates. The county's legal services advocates were grappling with increased caseloads as students overloaded the juvenile justice courts. Barbara Briggs, director of the Educational Advocacy Project for the Legal Aid Society of Palm Beach County, saw policing spike sharply after the Columbine incident: "That started the zero tolerance language. And from zero tolerance for students with weapons, it really morphed to zero tolerance for behavior typical of adolescents." . . .

At the national level, a 5-year-old coalition of legal, education, and community groups known as the Dignity in Schools

Campaign has been pushing for reforms to NCLB [No Child Left Behind] that would replace zero tolerance with alternatives and de-emphasize high-stakes testing. Last spring the coalition lobbied in Washington, D.C., for federal funding to support restorative justice and schoolwide positive behavioral supports to reduce suspensions and end the school-to-prison pipeline.

Students and their advocates face a long struggle to change the culture of school discipline that relies so heavily on law enforcement and criminal justice system strategies. But for young activists, reforming public schools and dismantling the school-to-prison pipeline created by zero tolerance may become the civil rights struggle of their generation.

"We want students to feel safe and encouraged to come to school," said Gonzalez. "An environment that has police and armed security guards and locked gates—that doesn't make us feel safe. The reality is that cops criminalize students for every little thing. For me it's violating our human rights because it's such a hostile place."

Periodical and Internet Sources Bibliography

The following articles have been chosen to supplement the diverse views presented in this chapter.

Marian Wright Edelman — "Zero Tolerance School Discipline Policies: A Failing Idea," August 5, 2011. www.childrensdefense.org.

Sabrina Rubin Erdely — "One Town's War on Gay Teens," *Rolling Stone*, February 2, 2012. www.rollingstone.com.

Nancy Gibbs — "Zero Tolerance: Zero Sense," *Time*, March 13, 2011. www.time.com.

Erica Goode — "Many in U.S. Are Arrested By Age 23, Study Finds," *New York Times*, vol. 19, December 2011.

Peter Katel — "Juvenile Justice: Are Sentencing Policies Too Harsh?," *CQ Researcher*, 2011.

Daniel J. Losen — "Discipline Policies, Successful Schools, and Racial Justice," 2011. www.nepc.colorado.edu.

Nirvi Shah — "Study Punctures Stereotypes About Social Status of Bullies," *Education Week*, vol. 30, no. 21, February 23, 2011.

Irene Sullivan — "Keeping Kids Outside the System: Alternatives to Juvenile Detention Are Cheaper and More Effective," *Reason*, vol. 43, no. 3, July 2011.

Anna Louie Sussman — "Suspension Trap," *The Progressive*, vol. 75, no. 4, April 2011.

Eugene Volokh — "Zero Tolerance," February 4, 2011. www.theconstitutional.org.

John W. Whitehead — "Zero Tolerance Schools Discipline Without Wiggle Room," *Huffington Post*, February 8, 2011. www.huffingtonpost.com.

For Further Discussion

Chapter 1

1. David Dobbs suggests that risk-taking behavior peaks during the late teen years, but these behaviors are actually a positive phase of development for teens and prepare them to leave home. Yet he concedes that this kind of teen behavior results in high accident rates. Do you agree with his conclusion that risk-taking behavior is ultimately a healthy thing for developing teenagers?

2. Craig A. Anderson concludes that playing violent video games contributes to aggression and violent behavior among teens. In contrast, Serena Gordon reports that a causal connection between playing violent video games and violent behavior has not been proven. How do you account for their different conclusions? Which viewpoint do you find more persuasive, and why?

Chapter 2

1. Reporter Jann Gumbiner argues that, compared to other drugs, marijuana is relatively harmless and seldom leads to the problems associated with substance abuse. Do the data cited by Gumbiner undermine CASA's argument? Why or why not?

2. As the National Institute on Drug Abuse points out, marijuana use seems to cause problems with memory and coordination, and it is associated with other health problems as well. Kristen Gwynne observes that teen marijuana use seems to be going up while teen alcohol and tobacco use are declining. She contends that the increase in marijuana use could be interpreted as a positive development. Which viewpoint do you find more persuasive, and why?

3. Michelle Minton contends that the minimum legal drinking age of twenty-one unfairly discriminates against young

people, leading a huge percentage of teens to break the law. She argues that the drinking age of twenty-one actually promotes the most dangerous kind of drinking: binge drinking. In contrast, Carla T. Main argues that lowering the drinking age would lead to more binge drinking, and the laws concerning underage drinking need to be enforced more strictly. If the drinking age were lowered, do you believe binge drinking would increase or decrease? In your opinion, would stronger punishments for underage drinking reduce teen drinking?

Chapter 3

1. David Crary argues that sexual harassment and bullying are pervasive in US middle and high schools. CBS News contends that as many as 25 percent of teens have experienced some form of cyberbullying. Are these serious problems in your school? After recent media attention to these problems, is the situation getting better or worse in your school?

2. Alean Zeiler contends that sex education emphasizing abstinence until marriage is the only truly effective form of sex education, because pregnancy and sexually transmitted diseases cannot result. Patrick Malone and Monica Rodriguez, in contrast, argue that comprehensive sex education, which emphasizes contraceptive techniques, is much more practical and effective. Which position do you find more persuasive? Explain your answer.

Chapter 4

1. Kenneth Miller makes a connection between the suicides of numerous gay teens and the anti-gay bullying they experienced. While acknowledging the connection between bullying and gay suicide, Jessica Bennett contends that the bullies in these cases should not go to jail—that other factors besides bullying are always involved. Do you find Bennett's

argument persuasive? Or should bullying that is a factor in suicide be punished more severely than it currently is?

2. Ken Trump argues that school zero tolerance policies have been unfairly criticized, and most school administrators are fair, even lenient, in their disciplinary policies. In contrast, Annette Fuentes contends that far too many students nation-wide are sent out of school into the legal system for minor offenses, and zero tolerance policies unfairly discriminate against students of color. Does your school system have a zero tolerance discipline policy? Is the policy applied to minor offenses as well as to serious offenses? Based on these two viewpoints, do you find zero tolerance policies to be necessary, or are they unfair?

Organizations to Contact

The editors have compiled the following list of organizations con-cerned with the issues debated in this book. The descriptions are derived from materials provided by the organizations. All have publications or information available for interested readers. The list was compiled on the date of publication of the present volume; the information provided here may change. Be aware that many organizations take several weeks or longer to respond to inquiries, so allow as much time as possible.

Advocates for Youth
200 M Street NW, Suite 750
Washington, DC 20036
(202) 419-3420 • fax: (202) 419-1448
website: www.advocatesforyouth.org

Advocates for Youth, founded in 1980, is dedicated to edu-cating and empowering young people to make responsible choices about their reproductive and sexual health. It advo-cates a positive, realistic approach to adolescent sexual health, focusing on young people ages fourteen to twenty-five. Among the organization's many publications are the pamphlets *Respect Yourself, Protect Yourself* and *I Think I Might Be Gay, Now What Do I Do?*

American Academy of Child and Adolescent Psychiatry (AACAP)
3615 Wisconsin Avenue NW
Washington, DC 20016-3007
(202) 966-7300 • fax: (202) 966-2891
website: www.aacap.org

AACAP is a non-profit, professional medical association dedi-cated to promoting mentally healthy children and adolescents through research, education, advocacy, diagnosis, and treatment.

It provides information to parents and families concerning the behavioral and mental disorders that affect children and adolescents. The AACAP publication series *Facts for Families* includes recent reports on topics such as bullying, childhood obesity, substance abuse, depression, and teen suicide.

American Civil Liberties Union (ACLU)

125 Broad Street
New York, NY 10004
(212) 549-2500
e-mail: aclu@aclu.org
website: www.aclu.org

A national organization founded in 1920, the ACLU is dedicated to defending the individual rights and liberties of all Americans through education, legal action, and advocacy. The ACLU takes positions on many issues relevant to teens, including sex education, juvenile justice, and discrimination based on sexual orientation. Recent articles include: "Students Have Privacy Rights Too," "Lift Children Out of the Juvenile Justice System—Don't Lock Them Away," and "Know Your Rights: A Quick Guide for LGBT High School Students."

Children's Defense Fund

23 E Street NW
Washington, DC 20001
(800) CDF-1200, (800) 233-1200
e-mail: cdfinfo@childrensdefense.org
website: www.childrensdefense.org

The Children's Defense Fund advocates for improvement in the health, education, and well-being of the nation's children and youth through a wide array of campaigns, programs, and publications. One prominent program is the CDF Freedom Schools, which provides summer and after-school enrichment opportunities for poor and minority students. Recent publications of the

CDF include the reports "Protect Children, Not Guns 2012," and "Walking While Black."

Choose Responsibility

PO Box 284
Ardsley-on-Hudson, NY 10503
(202) 543-8760 • fax: (202) 543-8764
e-mail: info@chooseresponsibility.org
website: www.chooseresponsibility.org

Choose Responsibility is a non-profit organization focused on the problems associated with youth alcohol consumption in the United States. The organization promotes awareness of the hazards of excessive and reckless drinking by US youth, and it advocates education, licensing, and a lower drinking age as solutions. Choose Responsibility was founded in 2007 by John M. McCardell Jr., former president of Middlebury College. Its original statement of purpose, called the Amethyst Initiative, has been signed by more than one hundred college presidents.

Coalition for Juvenile Justice (CJJ)

1710 Rhode Island Avenue NW, 10th Floor
Washington, DC 20036
(202) 467-0864 • fax: (202) 887-0738
e-mail: info@juvjustice.org
website: www.juvjustice.org

The Coalition for Juvenile Justice is a national nonprofit organization dedicated to reducing juvenile delinquency and improving the experience of youth who do enter the juvenile justice system. CJJ operates as an educational, training, and advocacy organization, and it provides numerous fact sheets, reports, and position papers. Recent position papers include: "Unequal Treatment of Minority Youth in the Juvenile Justice System" and "Positive Youth Justice: Framing Justice Interventions Using the Concepts of Positive Youth Development."

The Drug Policy Alliance

4455 Connecticut Avenue NW, Suite B-500
Washington, DC 20008-2328
(202) 537-5005 • fax: (202) 537-3007
website: www.drugpolicy.org

The mission of the Drug Policy Alliance is to reform current drug laws and policies through education and advocacy. It contends that the current war on drugs does more harm than good, particularly to young people and people of color who are disproportionately affected. Recent reports from the DPA include: "Safety First: a Reality-Based Approach to Teens and Drugs" and "Beyond Zero Tolerance: A Reality-Based Approach to Drug Education and School Discipline."

Family Research Council

801 G Street NW
Washington, DC 20001
(202) 393-2100 • fax: (202) 393-2134
website: www.frc.org

The Family Research Council, founded in 1983, is a conservative public policy and advocacy organization that promotes traditional views of marriage, sexuality, and family. It promotes the view that family values have been compromised in recent years at the hands of the federal government and liberal organizations. Among its many publications are articles opposing abortion, articles promoting abstinence sex education for teens, and articles opposing homosexuality as "unnatural" and harmful to society.

The Heritage Foundation

214 Massachusetts Avenue NW
Washington, DC 20002-4999
(202) 546-4400 • fax: (202) 546-8328
website: www.heritage.org

Founded in 1973, the Heritage Foundation is a research, educational, and advocacy organization dedicated to conservative principles as they pertain to government, economics, and social issues. Its target audience is Congress, policy makers, the media, and academia. On issues relevant to teens, the foundation has recently published such reports as "Evidence on the Effectiveness of Abstinence Education: An Update" and "Marriage: America's Greatest Weapon Against Child Poverty."

National Campaign to Prevent Teen and Unplanned Pregnancy

1776 Massachusetts Avenue NW, Suite 200
Washington, DC 20036
(202) 478-8500 • fax: (202) 478-8588
website: www.thenationalcampaign.org

The goal of the National Campaign to Prevent Teen and Unplanned Pregnancy is to reduce the number of teen and unplanned pregnancies in order to improve the lives and future prospects of US youth and families. Through education and advocacy, the organization works to ensure that children are born into stable, two-parent families rather than to single, young adults. Recent articles include: "Talking Back: Ten Things Teens Want Adults to Know About Teen Pregnancy" and "That's What He Said: What Guys Think About Sex, Love, Contraception, and Relationships."

National Center on Addiction and Substance Abuse at Columbia University (CASA)

633 Third Avenue, 19th Floor
New York, NY 10017-6706
(212) 841-5200
website: www.casacolumbia.org

The National Center on Addiction and Substance Abuse aims to transform society's attitudes toward substance use and addiction through research, education, and policy analysis. Founded in 1992, CASA addresses all forms of substance abuse, including alcohol, nicotine, and both legal and illegal drugs. Among its recent reports are: "National Survey of American Attitudes on Substance Abuse XVI: Teens and Parents" and "Adolescent Substance Use: America's #1 Public Health Problem."

National Institute on Drug Abuse (NIDA)
The National Institutes of Health
Bethesda, MD 20892-9561
(301) 443-1124
e-mail: information@nida.nih.gov
website: www.drugabuse.gov

As part of the National Institutes of Health, NIDA sponsors wide-ranging research on the problems of drug abuse and addiction, and it disseminates the results of that research to policy-makers and the general public in order to improve prevention and treatment. The website NIDA for Teens (www.teens.drug abuse.org) focuses on issues relevant to teenagers. Recent publications include: "Drugs: Shatter the Myths" and "Marijuana: Facts for Teens."

Parents, Families, and Friends of Lesbians and Gays (PFLAG)
1828 L Street NW, Suite 660
Washington, DC 20036
(202) 467-8180 • fax: (202) 349-0788
e-mail: info@pflag.org
website: www.pflag.org

A national non-profit organization, PFLAG promotes the health and well-being of all lesbian, gay, bisexual, and transgender persons through support services, education, and advocacy. PFLAG celebrates diversity and works to achieve a society that embraces everyone, regardless of sexual orientation or gender identity. Among the publications provided by PFLAG are *Be*

Yourself: Questions and Answers for Gay, Lesbian, Bisexual, and Transgender Youth and *Our Daughters and Sons: Questions and Answers for Parents of Gay, Lesbian, and Bisexual People.*

Planned Parenthood Federation of America (PPFA)
434 West 33rd Street
New York, NY 10001
(212) 541-7800 • (212) 245-1845
website: www.plannedparenthood.org

Planned Parenthood, the nation's largest sexual and reproductive health care provider and advocate, seeks to provide affordable, high quality reproductive health care at its clinics throughout the United States. The organization promotes comprehensive sex education, including contraceptive counseling and services, and it provides screening for cancer and testing for sexually transmitted infections. Publications include the pamphlets *Birth Control Choices for Teens* and *Teen Sex? It's Okay to Say No Way.*

Sexuality Information and Education Council of the United States (SIECUS)
130 W. 42nd Street, Suite 350
New York, NY 10036-7802
(212) 819-9770 • fax: (212) 819-9776
website: www.siecus.org

Since its founding in 1964, SIECUS has been a leading advocate of comprehensive sex education and a proponent of individual freedom concerning sexual and reproductive choices. Through its SexEdLibrary, SIECUS has long been a provider of sex education resources and lesson plans to educators. Its curricula have been endorsed by the Centers for Disease Control and Prevention (CDC). Recent publications include the booklet *Talk About Sex?* and the fact sheet "'I Swear I Won't': A Brief Explanation of Virginity Pledges."

Bibliography of Books

Joseph Allen and
Claudia Worrell
Allen

Escaping the Endless Adolescence.
New York: Ballantine Books,
2009.

Mark Bauerlein

*The Dumbest Generation: How
the Digital Age Stupefies Young
Americans and Jeopardizes Our
Future.* New York: Tarcher, 2008.

Donna J. Cornett

*Beat Binge Drinking: A Smart
Drinking Guide for Teens, College
Students and Young Adults Who
Choose to Drink.* Santa Rosa, CA:
People Friendly Books, 2011.

Michael A. Corriero

*Judging Children as Children:
A Proposal for a Juvenile Justice
System.* Philadelphia: Temple
University Press, 2006.

Kathi A. Earles and
Sandra E. Moore

*Scale Back: Why Childhood
Obesity Is Not Just About Weight.*
Chicago: Hilton, 2008.

Annette Fuentes

*Lockdown High: When the
Schoolhouse Becomes a Jailhouse.*
New York: VersoBooks, 2011.

Gina Guddat

*Unwrapped: Real Questions
Asked by Real Girls (About Sex).*
Houston TX: Providence, 2007.

Stephen Hinshaw
with Rachel Krantz

*The Triple Bind: Saving Our
Teenage Girls from Today's
Pressures.* New York: Ballantine
Books, 2009.

Kelly Huegel

GLBTQ: The Survival Guide for Gay, Lesbian, Bisexual, Transgender, and Questioning Teens. Minneapolis, MN: Free Spirit Publishing, 2011.

Matt Ivester

lol . . . OMG!: What Every Student Needs to Know About Online Reputation Management, Digital Citizenship and Cyberbullying. CreateSpace, 2011.

Thomas A. Jacobs

Teen Cyberbullying Investigated: Where Do Your Rights End and Consequences Begin? Minneapolis, MN: Free Spirit Publishing, 2010.

KidsPeace

I've Got This Friend Who: Advice for Teens and Their Friends on Alcohol, Drugs, Eating Disorders, Risky Behavior and More. Center City, MN: Hazelden, 2007.

Catherine Kim, Daniel Losen, and Damon Hewitt

The School-to-Prison Pipeline. New York: NYU Press, 2010.

Robin M. Kowalski, Susan P. Limber, and Patricia W. Agatston

Cyberbullying: Bullying in the Digital Age. Hoboken, NJ: Wiley-Blackwell, 2012.

Lawrence Kutner and Cheryl K. Olson

Grand Theft Childhood: The Surprising Truth About Violent Video Games. New York: Simon & Schuster, 2008.

Elizabeth Magill, ed.	*Drug Information for Teens: Health Tips About the Physical and Mental Effects of Substance Abuse.* Aston, PA: Omnigraphics, Inc., 2011.
Mike Males	*Teenage Sex and Pregnancy: Modern Myths, Unsexy Realities.* Santa Barbara, CA: Praeger, 2010.
Courtney E. Martin	*Perfect Girls, Starving Daughters: The Frightening New Normalcy of Hating Your Body.* New York: Free Press, 2007.
Jane McGonigal	*Reality is Broken: Why Games Make Us Better and How They Can Change the World.* New York: Penguin, 2011.
Pedro A. Noguera	*The Trouble With Black Boys and Other Reflections on Race, Equity, and the Future of Public Education.* San Francisco: Jossey-Bass, 2008.
Garrett Peck	*The Prohibition Hangover: Alcohol in America from Demon Rum to Cult Cabernet.* Piscataway, NJ: Rutgers University Press, 2009.
Mark D. Regnerus	*Forbidden Fruit: Sex & Religion in the Lives of American Teenagers.* New York: Oxford University Press, 2007.
Marsha Rosenbaum	*Safety First: A Reality-Based Approach to Teens and Drugs.* San Francisco: Drug Policy Alliance, 2007.

Dan Savage and
Terry Miller, eds.

It Gets Better: Coming Out, Overcoming Bullying, and Creating a Life Worth Living. New York: Dutton, 2011.

Wendy Shalit

Girls Gone Mild: Young Women Reclaim Self-Respect and Find It's Not Bad to Be Good. New York: Random House, 2007.

Don Tapscott

Grown Up Digital: How the Net Generation Is Changing Your World. New York: McGraw-Hill, 2009.

Jessica Valenti

The Purity Myth: How America's Obsession with Virginity Is Hurting Young Women. Berkeley, CA: Seal Press, 2009.

Index

A

Abortion rates, 105, 106, 127
Abrams, Douglas, 161
Abstinence-only-until-marriage, 15, 127–133, 135
Abstinence sex education, 106, 111–127
Academic performance, 67–68
Accidental deaths, 67–68
AIDS. *See* HIV/AIDS
Adaptive-adolescent story, 24–25, 27–29
Advanced Placement classes, 19
Advancement Project, 170, 173
African Americans
abortion rates, 105
in juvenile detention, 157
obesity rates, 31, 34
as superpredators, 169
zero tolerance policies and, 171
Aggravated assault, 48
Aggression
aggravated assault and homicide, 48
emotional desensitization to, 47
in justice system, 138
in marijuana smokers, 80
violent video games do not promote, 52–55
violent video games promote, 43–51
Alcohol use/abuse
availability, 18
beer drinking, 19, 94, 100
drinking and driving, 67, 98–100
media impact on, 69
obesity factors, 32

rates, 61, 84
See also Binge drinking; Minimum drinking age
Allen, Claudia Worrell, 19, 160
Allen, Joseph, 19, 160
Altruistic behavior, 23
American Association of University Women, 108–110
American College of Pediatricians, 120–122, 124
American Diabetes Association, 34
American Medical Association, 31
American Psychological Association (APA), 171
Amethyst Initiative, 92, 96–97, 99, 102
Anderson, Craig A., 43–51
Annie E. Casey Foundation, 156–162
Anti-bullying laws, 150–151
Anxiety
medication for, 89
from stress, 18
substance abuse and, 62, 71, 75, 79–80
Aristotle, 22
Arrest rates of juveniles, 59, 138, 158, 173
Associated Press, 18–19
Associated Press-MTV (AP-MTV) poll, 112–113, 116
Asthma, 51, 62, 68
Automobile-safety technologies, 93

B

Baird, Abigail, 24, 27
Bauerlein, Mark, 15
Beer drinking, 19, 94, 100

Bennett, Jessica, 148–155
Billitteri, Thomas J., 152
Binge drinking
    brain damage from, 68
    drinking age and, 100–101
    intoxication from, 99
    as underground culture, 92, 97
Bond, Bill, 110
Boston Globe (newspaper), 153
Brain
    damage from binge drinking, 68
    function changes with violent
        video games, 53
    impaired functioning, 62
    Marijuana effect on, 75–76,
        80–81
    reorganization of, 23
    reward system of, 75
Brain-imaging technology, 22
Brame, Robert, 138
Breaking Schools' Rules study,
    170–171
Briggs, Barbara, 173
Brooklyn College, 140
Brown, Asher, 140
Browne-Dianis, Judith, 170, 173
Bullying
    anti-bullying laws, 150–151
    cyberbullying, 111–116, 152
    to death, 149–150
    felony charges for, 153–154
    law is not deterrent to, 155
    as sexual harassment, 109
    should not be a crime, 148–155
    understanding, 151–153
    See also Gay teens and bullying
Buzzelli, Merle Bennett, 141,
    145–146

C
Caloric consumption, 35
Cannabis. *See* Marijuana use

Cardiovascular risk factors, 34, 68,
    78
Casey, B.J., 25, 27
Caucasians, 31, 34, 157
CBS News, 111–116
Centers for Disease Control and
    Prevention (CDC)
    contraception failure rates, 134
    STI rates, 118
    teen pregnancy declines, 105
    weight problems, 31
    Youth Risk Behavior
        Surveillance Survey by, 135
Chanon, Angeles, 154
Child neglect and abuse, 63
Choose Responsibility organiza-
    tion, 96
Cigarette smoking
    health impact, 68
    nicotine addiction, 62–63, 65,
        66–67, 71, 80
    rates, 61, 66, 84
    tobacco use/abuse, 32, 58, 67
    toxins, 65, 79
Clementi, Tyler, 140, 144, 149–150,
    152, 155
Clinton, Bill, 128, 169
Cocaine use, 61, 63, 71, 88
Columbine High School massacre,
    18, 169, 173
Comprehensive sexuality
    education programs, 128–129,
    132–133
Contraception use, 105–106, 120,
    128–129, 133–134
Costello, Maureen, 145
Counter-Strike (online game), 41
Crary, David, 107–110
Crimes by teens, 63, 138, 152
Cultural factors in addiction, 64
Cutting behavior, 19

Cyber junkies
  fantasy relationships of, 41–42
  gaming and internet trap, 38–39
  video game addiction signs,
    38–40
Cyberbullying, 111–116, 152
Cyberbullying Research Center,
  114, 155

D

Davis, Deon, 141–143
Davis, Rashad, 141
de Lara, Ellen, 143
DeMuro, Paul, 161
Dennis, Tracy, 53, 55
Depression, 32, 62, 119–120
*Derailed! The Schoolhouse to
  Jailhouse Track* (Browne-Dianis),
  173
Devine, Catherine, 112, 113
Diabetes, 33–34, 51
Digital generation, 14
Dignity in Schools Campaign,
  173–174
Dilulio, John, 169
Dirscherl, Dan, 93
Discrimination, 32, 92–93
Dishion, Tom, 160
Dobbs, David, 20–29
"Don't Ask, Don't Tell," 140
Draft age, 97–98
Dragan, Edward F., 115
Drug Abuse Resistance Education
  (DARE), 58–59
Drug-Free Schools and
  Communities Act (1986), 169
Drunk driving, 67, 98–100
Duke University, 96
*The Dumbest Generation: How
  the Digital Age Stupefies Young
  Americans and Jeopardizes Our
  Future* (Bauerlein), 15

Dysfunctional traits, 25

E

Eating disorders, 19
Emotional desensitization to ag-
  gression, 47
Erikson, Erik, 22
Ethical behavior, 23
EverQuest (online game), 41
Exodus International, 145
Experienced drinker hypothesis,
  93

F

Facebook, 38, 41, 113, 149, 153
Family Acceptance Project,
  142–143
Fantasy relationships, 41–42
Feinstein, Sheryl, 18
Finkelstein, Eric A., 30–36
Florida Atlantic University, 114
Florida Gulf Coast University, 142
*Forbidden Fruit: Sex & Religion in
  the Lives of American Teenagers*
  (Regnerus), 15
Fowler, Deborah, 138
Freud, Sigmund, 22
Fuentes, Annette, 168–174
Functional magnetic resonance
  imaging (fMRI), 53–54, 76

G

Gallup poll, 58, 140
Garbarino, James, 143
Gay-straight alliance groups, 140
Gay teens and bullying
  community support against,
    145–146
  homophobia, 140–141, 143
  parental power over, 141–142
  pressure of gender norms, 141
  safe environment against,
    146–147

as serious problem, 139–147
supporting gay teens, 142–144
tolerance and, 144–145
Gender norms, 141
Generalized forgetting effects, 88–89
Germany, 85, 93
Giedd, Jay, 26, 121
Goldberg, Sam, 155
Golden Rule Pledge, 145
Gordon, Serena, 52–55
Graves, Fatima Goss, 109
Gumbiner, Jann, 70–73
Guttmacher Institute, 105
Gwynne, Kristen, 82–89

H
Harrington, Zach, 144
Harvard School of Public Health
College Alcohol Study (CAS), 100–101
Hawkins, Kristan, 106
Health concerns
from addictions, 67–68
caloric consumption, 35
cardiovascular risk factors, 34, 68, 78
from underage drinking, 99
See also Alcohol use/abuse;
Cigarette smoking; Marijuana
use; Substance abuse; *and specific diseases/conditions*
Heart attack, 33, 63, 78
Heroin use, 71, 88
Herpes virus, 118
Hill, Catherine, 108
Hinduja, Sameer, 114, 155
Hispanics
abortion rates, 105
in juvenile detention, 157
obesity rates, 31
as superpredators, 169

zero tolerance policies and, 171
Homicide, 48, 67–68
Homophobia, 140–141
Homosexuality. *See* Gay teens and
bullying; Lesbian, gay, bisexual,
transgender (LGBT)
Huckaby, Jody M., 141
HIV/AIDS
contraception and, 134–135
gay teen risk for, 144
risks, 118–119
sex education and, 127–128
Human Papilloma Virus (HPV), 118–119
Hunter College, 53
Hyde, Margaret O., 65

I
Illegal drugs, 18, 61, 183
Impaired brain function, 62
Impulse control, 23, 64
Indiana University School of
Medicine, 53
Infertility concerns, 118
Inside the Teenage Brain
(Feinstein), 18
Insta-vigilantism, 151
Institute for the Study of Labor, 85
Internet
Facebook, 38, 41, 113, 149, 153
increased use of, 14–16
insta-vigilantism, 151
online multiplayer gaming, 15
See also Cyberbullying
Iowa State University, 116
Iverson, Leslie L., 71

J
Johnston, Lloyd, 86–87, 89
Journal of Adolescent Health (magazine), 140
Juvenile arrest rates, 59, 138, 158, 173

Juvenile detention
    changing views on, 159–161
    does not reduce crime, 158–159
    as ineffective, 156–162
    peer-based treatment programs
        against, 160
    reliance on, 157–158

K
Keefe, Colin, 155
Kenney, Kylie, 115
Kerlikowske, R. Gil, 85, 86
Kidney failure, 33
Kirby, Douglas, 132
Knowledge Networks, 110
Kost, Kathryn, 105
Krisberg, Barry, 161

L
Legal Aid Society of Palm Beach
    County Educational Advocacy
    Project, 173
Leone, Peter, 173
Lesbian, gay, bisexual, transgender
    (LGBT), 129, 130, 135
    See also Gay teens and bullying
Life expectancy decline, 32–35,
    33
LifeNews, 106
Lightner, Candace, 98
Lightner, Cari, 98
Longe, Ashley, 151
Los Angeles Times (newspaper),
    86
LSD, 88
Lucas, Billy, 140, 141
Ludwig, David, 32–34
Lung cancer, 48, 65, 68, 79
Lynn, Bob, 91
Lyons, Tiffany, 113

M
Main, Carla T., 95–102

Malone, Patrick, 126–135
Marijuana use
    addiction, 70–73, 80
    as beneficial, 85–86
    consequences, 78–79
    controlling synthetic marijuana,
        86–87
    education needs over, 86
    effect on brain, 75–76, 80–81
    as harmful, 71–81
    as harmless, 66
    health impact, 68, 78
    medical marijuana, 72, 85
    memory impairment, 76–79
    over more harmful substances,
        82–89
    perceptions of harm, 84–85
    rates, 58, 61, 67, 84
    regulating intake, 72–73
    respiratory problems with,
        79–80
    risks, 77, 83–84
    for stress relief, 19
    tetrahydrocannabinol (THC)
        levels, 72, 75, 76
Mathematica Policy Research, 124,
    131–132
Mayer, Matthew, 173
McCardell, John M., 92, 96
McCrimmon, Katie Kerwin, 77
McGonigal, Jane, 15
Media impact on substance abuse,
    69
Media violence, 47–49
Medical marijuana, 72, 85
Mendel, Richard A., 156–162
Methamphetamines, 84, 86, 88
Middlebury College, 92, 96
Miller, Kenneth, 139–147
Minimum drinking age
    binge drinking and, 100–101

in college, 101–102
drunk driving link, 98–100
enforcement, 102
removing allure of drinking, 97
selection of, 91–92
should be lowered, 90–94
should not be lowered, 95–102
traffic fatality link, 93–94
as twenty one, 97–99
underground drinking culture,
92–93
Minton, Michelle, 90–94
Mom, Dad, I'm Gay: How Families Negotiate Coming Out (Savin-Williams), 143
Monitoring the Future survey, 58, 83
Mothers Against Drunk Driving (MADD), 92, 98
Moving away from home, 28–29
MTV, 18–19, 112, 113, 116
Mulveyhill, Sean, 151, 154
Myst (video game), 51

N
National Academy of Sciences, 59
National Association of Secondary School Principals, 110
National Center for Education Statistics, 169
National Center for Higher Education Risk Management, 101
National Center for Juvenile Justice, 59
National Center on Addiction and Substance Abuse, 58, 60–69
National Council on Crime and Delinquency, 161
National District Attorneys Association, 153
National Institute on Drug Abuse (NIDA), 74–81, 83, 86, 92

National Institutes of Health (NIH), 23, 26, 92–93
National Minimum Drinking Age Act (1984), 91
National Survey on Drug Use and Health (NSDUH), 80
National Women's Law Center, 109
Nelson, Toben F., 100
New York Times (newspaper), 85, 93
New York University, 110
Newsweek (magazine), 153, 154
Nicotine addiction, 62–63, 65, 66–67, 71, 80
Nixon, Richard, 58
No Child Left Behind (NCLB), 174

O
Obama, Barack, 112
Obesity
caloric consumption, 35
defined, 31
discrimination link, 32
disease risks, 34–35
food options promote, 30–36
life expectancy decline with, 32–34, *33*
public school foods, 35–36
rising rates, 31–32
Observational learning, 45
Office of Drug Control Policy, 58
Olweus, Dan, 151
Omaha South High Magnet School, 146
Online bullying. *See* Cyberbullying
Online multiplayer gaming, 15
The Other Parent: The Inside Story of the Media's Effect on Our Children (Steyer), 50
OxyContin, 88
Oxytocin hormone, 27

P

Pacific Institute for Research and Evaluation, 101

Parental expectations, 19, 69

Parents, Families, and Friends of Lesbians and Gays (PFLAG), 141, 142

Patchin, Justin W., 152

Pediatrics (journal), 138

Peer-based treatment programs, 160

Peer pressure
  bullying and, 150
  gender norms and, 141
  opinions based on, 12
  risky behavior with, 18–19, 21
  social pull, 27–28

Pelvic inflammatory disease (PID), 118

Pink Floyd (music group), 15

Police presence in schools, 171–173

Pornography, 15, 114

Prescription drug abuse, 61, 62, 64, 66, 69, 87–89

Presidents Against Drunk Driving, 92–93

Prince, Phoebe, 149, 150, 151–154

Psychosexual conflict, 22

Psychosis, 62

Public school foods, 35–36

Puzzanchera, Charles, 59

Q

Quasha, Scott, 140–141, 147

R

Radiological Society of North America, 53

Reagan, Ronald, 98, 169

Reality Is Broken: Why Games Make Us Better and How They Can Change the World (McGonigal), 15

Regnerus, Mark D., 15

Renaud, Austin, 151

Reyes, Augustina, 172

Riggs, Cara, 146

Roberts, Kevin, 37–42

Robertson, Pat, 58

Rodriguez, Monica, 126–135

RuneScape (online game), 41

Ryan, Caitlin, 142–144

S

Safe and Gun-Free Schools Act (1994), 169

San Francisco State University, 143

Savin-Williams, Ritch, 143

Sayer, Gus, 154

Scheibel, Elizabeth, 153

Schizophrenia-like disorders, 76

School Resource Officers (SROs), 165–166

School security programs, 165–166

School shootings, 47–48
  Columbine High School massacre, 18, 169, 173
  violent video games and, 47–48
  Virginia Tech massacre, 18

Sensation-seeking behavior, 25–26

Setaro, John F., 65

Sex education
  on abstinence, 106, 117–125
  abstinence-only-until-marriage, 15, 127–133, 135
  comprehensive sexuality education programs, 128–129, 132–133
  culture wars over, 127–128
  disease and pregnancy risks, 118–119
  government role, 124–125
  laws should mandate topics, 134–135
  medical accuracy with, 133–134

merits, 15
parental role, 121–123
problem with comprehensive
    programs, 123
protection and safety emphasis
    needed, 126–135
studies, 131–132
teen sex and trauma, 119–120
two approaches, 120–121,
    128–129
Sexting, 112, 114–116
Sexual harassment/assault
anonymous reporting, 110
bullying as, 109
is pervasive, 107–110
online, 15
rates, 68, 101
Sexual intercourse, 34, 120
Sexuality in teens
alcohol use among, 67
contraception use, 105–106,
    120, 128–129, 133
overview, 105–106
pornography and, 15
trauma link, 119–120
unprotected consensual sex, 101
Sexuality Information and
    Education Council of the United
    States (SIECUS), 123, 128
Sexually transmitted infections
    (STI), 118–120, 123, 129, 130
    See also HIV/AIDS
Shakespeare, William, 22
Shalit, Wendy, 122
The Sims (video game), 51
16 and Pregnant (TV show), 105
Skiba, Russell, 171
Smith, Dan, 153
Smoking. See Cigarette smoking
Social media, 14, 16, 19, 41–42
    See also Facebook

Social scene, 27–28
Social Security Act, 128, 129
Sokolow, Brett, 101–102
Southern Poverty Law Center, 145
Steinberg, Laurence, 26, 27
Steyer, James, 50
Students Against Destructive
    Decisions (SADD), 18
Substance abuse
addiction link, 62
addiction risks, 66–67
anxiety and, 62, 71, 75, 79–80
with cocaine, 61, 63, 71, 88
consequences, 62–63
does not lead to addiction,
    70–73
financial cost, 63
generalized forgetting effects,
    88–89
with heroin, 71, 88
with illegal drugs, 18, 61, 183
impact, 67–68, 69
leads to addiction, 60–69
making of an epidemic, 64–66
media impact, 69
with methamphetamine, 84,
    86, 88
overview, 58–59
with prescription drugs, 61, 62,
    64, 66, 69, 87–89
progress against has stalled, 66
for stress relief, 19
    See also Marijuana use
Suffolk Law School, 151
Sugar consumption, 35
Suicide risks, 19, 67–68, 112,
    119–120
Synthetic marijuana, 86–87

T
Teachable moment idea, 170
Teaching Tolerance project, 145

Teen Mom (TV show), 105
Teenage pregnancy
    abortion rates, 105–106, 127
    early onset of puberty link, 34
    impact, 119
    rates, 105, 130
    substance abuse link to, 62
Teens, risk-taking behavior
    brain adaptivity, 24–25
    brain reorganization, 23
    function of teenage brain,
        20–29
    at its peak, 26
    learning to use new network, 24
    moving away from home, 28–29
    mystery of, 22
    overview, 21–22
    risk vs. rewards, 27
    sensation-seeking behavior,
        25–26
    social scene pull, 27–28
Tegeder, Mike, 144–145
Temple University, 26
Tetrahydrocannabinol (THC) levels, 72, 75, 76
Throckmorton, Warren, 145, 146
Tobacco use/abuse, 32, 58, 67
Traffic fatalities, 93–94
Trump, Ken, 163–167
TV/film violence, 47

U
Underground drinking culture,
    92–93
Uniform Drinking Age Act (1984),
    98–99
University of California-Berkeley,
    161
University of Cambridge, 71
University of Houston, 172
University of Illinois at Chicago,
    32

University of Missouri, 161
University of Notre Dame, 93
University of Scranton, 113
Unprotected consensual sex, 101
US Department of Education, 59,
    112, 146, 169
US Department of Health and
    Human Services, 92, 124, 132
US Department of Justice, 169
US Food and Drug
    Administration, 87–88
US General Accounting Office, 59
US House of Representatives, 86,
    87
US Supreme Court, 92
US Surgeon General, 59

V
Velasquez, Sharon, 151, 154
Vending machine access in
    schools, 31–32
Verbal assaults, 151
Vicodin, 88
Video games
    addiction to, 39, 40
    early addiction signs, 38–39
    as escapism, 19
    rise of, 14–15
    secret gaming, 39–41
Vietnam War, 71, 97
Violent video games
    brain function changes with, 53
    debate over harm, 54
    do not promote aggression,
        52–55
    long-term impact, 46–47
    marketing, 50–51
    more research needed, 54–55
    negative effects, 47–50
    overview, 44–45
    promote aggression, 43–51
    short-term impact, 45–46, *46*

Virginia Tech massacre, 18
Voting age, 97

W
Walsh, Seth, 140, 146
Wang, Yang, 53–55
War on Drugs, 58
Waxman, Henry, 124
Way, Niobe, 110
Weapons in schools, *172*
Wechsler, Henry, 100
Weill Cornell Medical College, 25
*Why kNOw Abstinence Education
  Program Teacher's Manual,*
  133–134
Wilhelmi, Alec, 116
Wilson, James Q., 169
The Winter's Tale (Shakespeare), 22
World of Warcraft (online game),
  38–39, 41

Y
Yale Child Study Center, 170
Yamada, David, 151
Youth Risk Behavior Surveillance
  Survey, 135

Z
Zeiler, Alean, 117–125
Zero tolerance policies
  discriminatory aspects, 171
  enforcement, 138
  expansion, 169–170
  as harmful, 168–174
  is not to blame, 164
  leniency by school administra-
    tors and, 165
  over weapons in schools, *172*
  police presence in schools,
    171–173
  problems with exaggerated,
    163–167
  safety plans vs., 166–167
  school security programs,
    165–166
  suspensions skyrocketing with,
    170–171
Zogby Poll, 124
Zuckerman, Laurie, 30–36

CPSIA information can be obtained
at www.ICGtesting.com
Printed in the USA
FFOW030000080113
657FF

9 780737 764314